RESUSCITATING THE ALMOST DEAD

(Breathing New Life Into Your Church)

By Jeffrey M. Earman

Text copyright © 2013 Jeffrey M. Earman

Table of Contents

Introduction

Chapter 1 – Why Are Churches Ailing?   5

Chapter 2 – A Renewed Congregation   13

Chapter 3 – How to Breathe in New Life   19

Chapter 4 – Caution Signs   51

Chapter 5 – An Example of What Not to Do   55

Chapter 6 – The Winning Coach Analogy   57

Chapter 7 – Antagonists and Ms. Own-a-Pew   63

Chapter 8 – The Pastor as Leader   77

Chapter 9 – The "Change Agent" Pastor   89

Conclusion   102

INTRODUCTION

I have been in ministry for nearly thirty years. For twenty-two of those years I worked at revitalizing two small congregations. I know what it's like to pastor a struggling church and wonder if I can make a difference. There were many times when I felt discouraged and lonely. Like most pastors, I have made mistakes and learned from many trials and errors. Eventually, I began to see church attendance grow and positive changes occur.

It is exciting for a pastor to experience substantial growth in the church. However, if the church is in a small town or rural area, he may or may not see the congregation grow to a very large size. The role of the pastor is not to create a mega church, but to be faithful to God's calling and to do the work of the ministry. But with prayer and the application of principles of church growth, it is possible for his church to experience revitalization and growth.

Many of the ideas you will find here are just common sense. I include thirty-five suggestions and ideas that I have successfully used in bringing new life to a church. Because my small churches had limited budgets, you may note that I tried to operate "on a shoestring." Out of necessity, I learned to be creatively cheap. There are ways to save money in one area in order to invest in another.

Surprisingly, I learned many turn-around principles when I was in youth ministry. I was on the staff with the local Youth for Christ chapter for four years and I had been a youth pastor or sponsor at several churches. I found myself in situations where the church youth group or the YFC Campus Life Club had fallen on hard times. In each situation, I had to figure out how to "jump start" the youth ministry. Perhaps it was simple persistence but I experienced success every time.

In each church, I started out working part-time secular jobs (bi-vocational) until the church grew, because struggling congregations are usually unable to pay the pastor a full-time salary. Working a part-time job was not what I had envisioned for myself in seminary. Some of my fellow graduates felt sorry for me. Why in the world would he go to that little church? Perhaps I am crazy because I have a tendency to go where others won't go. I love a challenge and doing something that others say cannot be done. Even though I majored in Church Growth and Evangelism, the real classroom was "in the field." My friends and parishioners suggested that I write a book based on my experiences and share what worked for me.

Church growth principles have made a tremendous impact on my approach to church ministry. The subject of church revitalization is based on the idea that individual congregations can make changes that return them to vibrancy. However, we need to use caution when applying church growth principles. What works in one setting may fail miserably in another. There are wide differences between smaller local churches and the strategy used must be flexible, realistic, and basic.

Revitalization is more than growth in attendance, or having a big building, or a fat bank account, although these can be indicators of progress. The real measurement of revitalization is when hearts are changed, the congregation grows closer to Christ and a new sense of love and joy permeates the fellowship.

CHAPTER 1   WHY ARE CHURCHES AILING?

There are many reasons why a church becomes sick. Some churches can recuperate and some cannot. Others are on life support. It takes honest evaluation to determine if the disease is terminal. If a congregation wants to recover it must open to treatment. But first, there needs to be a diagnosis.

I know from experience that turning a church around is extremely hard work. A successful revitalizer needs the ability to diagnose properly the hindrances to growth and the wisdom to know how to implement changes to promote a growth environment. He will need spiritual fortitude, a positive attitude, leadership abilities, knowledge of church growth principles, a willingness to introduce change, and a backbone when facing dysfunctional people.

Struggling churches share common characteristics. Some of these are discussed below.

Difficult People. One particular negative characteristic is the presence of dysfunctional followers within the church. Frequently there are one or more individuals who are the cause of an unhealthy fellowship. They have created a negative and critical atmosphere.

In *Dying for Change*, Leith Anderson observes, "Some churches have members who are self-programmed to criticism, reaction, and disloyalty. They insist on clear and compelling reasons to override their negative defaults. Such churches can be impossible to lead. They are like computers with an internal destructive virus."

The make-up of the church members is vital. The pastor will need to determine who has influence over others in the group. Some will be responsible leaders who understand the measures necessary for change while others will have a negative opinion of any change. Often these established people are afraid to lose power and may view the new pastor as a threat to their influence.

The truth is that some of these people are a serious detriment to spiritual vitality in the fellowship and may need to be confronted. Bill Easum, a church growth consultant, states,

Being nice is not what Jesus wants from any of us. One of the basic lessons I'm learning as a consultant is that before renewal begins in a church or denomination, it is normal that someone has to leave or be denied. Almost every time a dying church attempts to thrive once again, someone tries to bully the leadership out of the attempt. And almost every time, if a turn around is to take place, such persons are lost along the way because they are no longer allowed to get their way. When they can't get their way, they leave.

The established people in the church may even like the pastor, but think he is too idealistic and immature to appreciate the church's rich tradition and the importance of certain individuals. Hopefully, as the pastor gains their confidence he can help them see that he only wants the best for the congregation. Anderson warns that the twenty-first century church has a revolution occurring in the world around it and it cannot afford to be caught up in petty differences. He is correct in saying, "Blessed is the church with followers who are willing to set aside their personal priorities and align with the greater priorities of the body."

Aging members are another problem facing the dying church. These small congregations were perhaps once dynamic but failed to make changes necessary for growth. As grown children move to find work, the congregation cannot replenish its leadership base. Wagner observes, "Old age is mostly a rural disease while ethnikitis is mostly urban. Some rural communities are getting smaller and smaller, businesses are closing, and family farms are being taken over by large agricorporations." There comes a time when some churches have finished the ministry to their generation and need to close.

This is unfortunate because the older congregation was a church plant years ago. There was a movement of God in the lives of individuals who decided to "start a church". Over time the dream faded, the founding pastor moved on, and the church's vision was forgotten.

Just because a congregation has gotten older does not mean that it cannot attract younger people. I think it all depends on the attitude of the membership. I have seen young pastors begin to attract young families only to have the aging members gripe about the noise the children are making. I have also seen older members making over children and loudly interacting with them. I know that my own children were often delighted by the love and attention they received from older people.

The Small Church is Often Ingrown. The members are a close-knit "family" who have become accustomed to operating a certain way. The same people perform the same functions every year. They are comfortable with the Sunday morning routine that has been in place for years: the order of the worship service, the music, the rituals and recitations, the length of the sermon and the places where people sit do not change.

Most congregations view themselves as being friendly and welcoming to the Sunday morning visitor. However, they think they are friendly because they are nice to each other. They often gather in little groups to greet their friends and ignore the visitor. The regular attendees do not make the effort to walk across the sanctuary to introduce themselves to people they don't know. The visitor can forget about being invited to a member's home for lunch.

John Miller has excellent insights into the problems facing the pastor. In his book, *Outgrowing the Ingrown Church*, he lists the following symptoms found in an ingrown church.

> *Tunnel Vision.* Members of the ingrown church body are characterized by tunnel vision that limits potential ministries of the church to those that can be accomplished by the visible, human resources at hand.
>
> *Shared Sense of Group Superiority.* They build an attitude of superiority by elevating a positive feature in the church life or tradition and then comparing this feature with groups that lack this quality.
>
> *Extreme Sensitivity to Negative Human Opinion.* The sad truth is that one negative critic with a loud voice who speaks from within the inner circle of the ingrown church usurps the role of Christ, wielding the power to make or break programs.

Niceness in Tone. What is often wanted in the local church is unrelieved blandness: a 'nice preacher' preaching a 'nice sermon' about a 'nice Jesus' delivered in a 'nice tone of voice'. What we really want is to be comfortable and undisturbed. Nice is just another way of being safe.

Christian Soap Opera in Style. The niceness of the inward-looking church does not go deep enough to hinder the soap-opera style in which many a congregational life is lived. Soap operas are basically a series of endlessly repeated conversations, and gossip is often the only kind of 'body life' an ingrown church knows.

Confused Leadership Roles. In many churches, the members of the congregation do not want officers who are trying to be pacesetters for God's kingdom. Zeal for Christ's global missionary cause in a leader is hard for old wine-skins to handle.

A Misdirected Purpose. It is clear that the controlling purpose of the ingrown church is survival - not growth through the conversion of the lost. We can recognize this misdirected purpose by noting what composes the church budget and how visitors to the church services are welcomed. Visitors to the inward-looking congregation may be given a formal welcome and a smile, but the heart is not in it. No planning is devoted to finding ways to assimilate visitors into the fellowship.

The ingrown church is in need of spiritual renewal. Just like individuals who "backslide" away from God, so do congregations. Hopefully, as more denominations discover the need for revitalization, leaders will check the spiritual temperature of their dying churches. One group in particular has accurately discerned why their churches are not growing. The Reformed Church in America (RCA) has identified seven barriers to revitalization in the Evangelism and Church Development Services Committee report to the General Synod. The report's analysis is right on target.

Demonic Divisions. The Bible is clear regarding the spiritual struggle and demonic dimension to the realization of the mission of the church. This is especially true of churches in need of revitalization.

Leadership Challenged. From inadequate pastoral training models, which have not produced ministers capable of leading the church, to laity who have not been equipped and encouraged to use their leadership gifts, the declining church faces a leadership challenge that is a significant barrier to the process of renewal.

No Passion for God. When there is no passion, no hunger or thirst for God, new life is illusive. Renewal may need to be preceded by repentance. This barrier can only be broken down through the power of the Holy Spirit.

Not Mission-Driven. A congregation's unwillingness or inability to communicate the gospel, to search out its biblical purpose and live it out accordingly is one of the greatest barriers to revitalization.

People Not Using Their Gifts. Turning a church around is blocked by the limiting of lay participation. The ministry must be entrusted to God's people, God's building made with living stones who can minister for God's glory.

Internal Focus. A major barrier to a church's revitalization efforts is a self-centered, internal focus that cares not for the people for whom God cares and for whom Jesus died on the cross, but instead communicates: "This church exists for me and my family, and to meet our needs."

Pastors and Lay Leaders Lack Christ-Like Authenticity. Unless pastors and lay leaders are willing to grow in their walk with God to a place of being living examples of the transforming power of Jesus Christ, they will be both stumbling blocks and barriers to the work of revitalization that God desires to do in the church.

Is it easier to birth a baby or resurrect the dead? Denominational leaders are looking for ways to help their many small non-growing churches and recognize that there are no easy solutions.

Rather than attempting to revitalize older and smaller churches, some denominations are finding it easier to plant new congregations instead. This is understandable since, as it has been said, "It is easier to birth a baby than to resurrect the dead." Experience bears this out when it comes to planting a new congregation versus entering an existing small congregation and confronting the barriers to growth.

The lack of interest in turning around congregations instead of planting new ones neglects an obvious opportunity for growth. Why are we not preparing more students for revitalization of non-growing churches since there are literally thousands of small churches already planted in the United States? Is it not possible for some of them to be led into renewed vision and growth?

Yet most pastors look for a placement at an existing church rather than plant a new one. Unfortunately, many of these pastors will enter a small church environment fresh out of seminary, filled with idealism and lots of class time, but no realistic preparation for what they will encounter. These new pastors will probably recognize the need for transforming their church and will look for ways to re-energize their congregation at seminars and conferences.

Pastors are not trained to lead. This is a problem because leadership is crucial to successful ministry. Most seminary professors are not leaders, much less experienced church pastors. I saw this in seminary. They have the teaching gift but not the leadership gift. As a result, they train students to be teachers, not leaders. In the past, the emphasis at many seminaries has been the "servant leadership" model, which does not stress taking the initiative. It fits the teacher gift rather than the leader gift. This model seems okay until we observe that most congregations are not growing due to a lack of vision on the part of the pastor. Dr. C. Peter Wagner notes,

> One reason why strong pastoral leadership is not characteristic of many of America's churches is that in the recent past clergy have been taught just the opposite in seminaries. They were taught to reject strong, authoritative, directive pastoral leadership.

It does not take long for a weak pastor to hurt the momentum of a church. Greg Jones, a professor at Duke Divinity School, made the observation that, "Strong congregations can survive mediocre or poor pastoral leadership, at least for a while. But over time, ineffective pastoral leaders weaken congregations, and weak congregations often attract pastors who reflect and perpetuate mediocrity. The relationship between congregation and pastor then spirals downward into mutual weakness."

Big shoes for little feet. Thousands of pastors attend conferences every year in search of answers for their church. Leaders want fresh ideas detailing how to transform their congregation, with all of its traditions, rules, and patterns, into the re-energized, vibrant church that they envision.

The church growth movement has spawned countless books and seminars about how increase church attendance. In some ways, the strategies taught by successful pastors have been most helpful. But church growth seminar schedules are usually loaded with speakers who pastor a "mega church" with whopping statistics printed in the seminar program. Some have congregations the size of small towns and staff the size of medium corporations. While it is acceptable to hold these successful pastors up as examples, we ought to consider what is transferable to the smaller church. The average pastor cannot relate to these large churches, much less implement all of their strategies in his setting. Of course, many plateaued churches can learn from large churches and grow using their ideas, but may never become the next Willow Creek or Saddleback. After all, a formula that works in one setting may not be universally successful.

Status quo pastors. At the other end of the spectrum are pastors who are comfortable with the status quo. This is a problem worldwide as too many pastors make excuses for the lack of growth in their congregations. Dr. Paul Cho recounts how he prayed for insight regarding why his churches were not growing. "After prayed, I was sure I had diagnosed the problem. These men were satisfied with the status quo. They had congregations of thirty to fifty members and since most tithed, they could live comfortably without expanding. So often churches become exclusive clubs. When this happens, the desire for church growth will not develop."

In order for the smaller church to grow some radical changes need to occur within the core group's thinking. One crucial area is the way the congregation views the function of the pastor. Too many churches treat the pastor like a chaplain whose job is to do nothing but preach and give them warm feelings so they can walk away happy. As noted by Carl F. George, "Over half the churches in America are 'nuzzle the shepherd' congregations. Usually they have an attendance of seventy-five weekly worshipers or less, and the majority have a warm relationship with the pastor."

Not all the blame can be placed at the feet of the laity. After all, how many pastors are happy to just give a little homily and go home rather than challenge their flock to become all God wants them to be? Carl George continues, "Although they may belong to the group that called you to lead their church, that is not really what they want you to do. Rather, they probably think they hired you to stand in their pulpit, lead the worship service, preach, help them raise their budget, handle weddings and funerals, and visit them in the hospital. In short, they frequently view the pastor as the chaplain or the hired hand."

What if the church members are not dying for change? Some congregations proudly hang on to certain traditions for tradition's sake and miss the movement of the Holy Spirit. The church can no longer stay within the confines of its little castle and hope someone will knock on the drawbridge door asking to visit.

CHAPTER 2   A RENEWED CONGREGATION

There are specific attributes found in congregations that have been revitalized. Some of the healthy signs of a revitalized church are spiritual renewal, expressions of love, enthusiastic worship, affirming leadership, a sense of purpose, and a higher level of lay involvement.

Spiritual vibrancy is an obvious sign that a congregation is healthy. Spiritual renewal refers to a fresh encounter with God, resulting in restored relationships and a new sense of *joy* in worship. The work of renewal is initiated by God and catalyzed by the Holy Spirit. Many people who attend have had a conversion experience or have experienced a spiritual re-awakening at the cross of Christ. They have a zealous walk with God that is reflected in time spent in Bible study and prayer, living out their faith with contagious enthusiasm, and a willingness to share the good news of Jesus Christ to others. They serve Christ through use of their spiritual gifts and acts of service. Christ centered hearts are at the core of who they are.

While he served as director of the *Southern Baptist Center for Church Growth*, Ken Hemphill studied growing churches and discovered that they had eight common characteristics:

> Growing churches have a profound awareness of the supernatural empowering of God to grow their church.

> Growing churches have a serious commitment to passionate prayer.

> The growing church experiences Christ-exalting worship.

> Growing churches are led by servant leaders. Leadership is a function while servanthood is an attitude.

> The healthy, growing church is marked by kingdom family relationships. Five relationships are important to a growth atmosphere: pastor to God, people to God, pastor to people, people to pastor, and people to people.

> The growing church is possessed by a God-sized vision, a vision communicated by God to people who are obedient to the Great Commission.

The distinguishing characteristic of the growing church is a passion for the lost.

Growing churches have a commitment to discipleship.

Authentic Christ-like love. There is a "love factor" in the fellowship. There is great joy and an expression of love. Churches experiencing renewal are committed to living out the love of Christ in accordance with Biblical teaching. They practice forgiveness. "If anyone says, 'I love God,' yet hates his brother, he is a liar. For anyone who does not love his brother whom he has seen, cannot love God whom he has not seen. And he has given us this command: Whoever loves God must also love his brother." (1 John 4:20-21)

These churches celebrate their life in Christ and engage in activities that build greater relationships. Their associations are characterized by a relatively high degree of sensitivity and caring both inside and outside the church fellowship. The relationships in the church are based on authenticity and trust. Visitors immediately sense the love of God when they enter the worship service. "This is the message you heard from the beginning: We should love one another." (1 John 3:11) "And he has given us this command: Whoever loves God must also love his brother." (1 John 4:21) Jesus said that by such love "all men will know you are my disciples." (John 13:34-35)

The first four of the Ten Commandments describe ways people could show their love to God by keeping Him first, by honoring Him, and by remembering Him. The remaining six commandments communicate love for people by doing them no harm but rather good. When the pastor preaches love for God and love for others, the church is going to grow because the fellowship will be sweet and members look forward to going to church on Sunday. The leadership is encouraging and positive.

Competent leadership and mission. Renewed congregations have pastoral leadership with a clear purpose and direction. Spiritual leadership is a key component in the revitalization process. The congregation appreciates a pastor who leads the congregation by equipping lay leaders to serve in the church. The leaders know their spiritual gifts and encourage others to discover their gifts, also. The pastor doing the entire ministry proves nothing. Gathering gifted people and equipping and unleashing them for ministry builds a stronger team base. The congregation rediscovers its purpose and embarks on a process of determining God's unique mission for them in the local community and the world. The church rallies around an articulated mission statement and has a profound sense of the reason for their church's existence.

Ministry decisions are consistent with the congregational purpose statement, which clarifies the purpose of each ministry. The congregations who desire relevance examine each program and ministry and are open to assess, evaluate, change and discontinue ministries that are no longer effective.

In his book, *One Size Does Not Fit All*, Gary McIntosh provides several practical suggestions that may help smaller congregations:

> *Renew a sense of purpose.* This begins by focusing the attention of the congregation on Jesus Christ, particularly his death on the cross.

> *Begin new ministries.* The ingrown fellowship in small churches is perpetuated by programs and ministries that have become saturated. Since most people prefer to be in on the ground floor of a new venture, beginning new ministries is an essential step to attract and hold newcomers. Think in terms of Events, Experiences, and Education. A crucial aspect of adding new ministries is adding a second worship service. Perhaps the number one way that a small church breaks out of its single cell orientation into multiple cell orientation is by adding a second worship service.

> *Cultivate evangelism.* Develop outreach events so members can invite the people they have been praying for over the year.

> *Start new groups and classes.* The creation of new groups and classes begins the process of moving from a single cell church to a multiple cell model of ministry. Add additional Sunday School classes.

Celebrate victories. Call attention to the positives in the church. Report the results of effective ministries. Talk more about strengths than weaknesses.

Involve new people. It is false to think that new people quickly develop a sense of belonging. Invite them to participate in key positions and ministries.

Growth can be encouraged by providing a positive environment, but we cannot make it happen ourselves. That is God's job. "So neither he who plants nor he who waters is anything, but only God, who makes things grow." (1 Corinthians 3:7)

A Biblical blueprint is followed. A church that in cooperates with God's design will grow. "For we are God's fellow workers; you are God's field, God's building." (1 Corinthians 3:9) I think the following conditions provide fertile ground for growth:

First, *all preaching and teaching is based on the Bible*. Both the means and the end of growth must be filtered through the lens of Scripture. Just because a tactic or program seems to work doesn't mean it is of God. God will never violate what He has already stated in His Word. (Hebrews 5:11-14 & II Timothy 3:16-17) Discipleship begins with Biblical studies. Either write or obtain a discipleship course that encompasses most of the basics such as prayer, temptation, personal evangelism, Christology, forgiveness, spiritual gifts, theological questions, daily walk with God, etc.

Second, *glorifying Jesus Christ must be central to our beliefs and practices*. Whatever is done must be done in the Lord's power and authority with the goal of honoring and pleasing Him. Growth will occur when we are more concerned that people encounter Jesus than that they have a good impression of our programs, our methods, our theological and philosophical bents, or us. Take note of the following Biblical references:

> For no one can lay any foundation other than the one already laid, which is Jesus Christ. (1 Corinthians 3:11)

And he is the head of the body, the church; he is the beginning and the firstborn from the dead, so that in everything he might have supremacy. (Colossians 1:18)

And whatever you do, whether in word or deed, do it all in the name of the Lord Jesus, giving thanks to God the Father through him. (Colossians 3:17)

Let us fix our eyes on Jesus, the author and perfecter of our faith, who for the joy set before him endured the cross, scorning its shame, and sat down at the right hand of the throne of God. (Hebrews 12:1-2)

Third, the church must build people up with the grace of God. Because in Christ there is no condemnation, we can encourage each other instead of comparing or competing with one another. Surrounded by grace (acceptance, forgiveness, affirmation, kindness), we then become motivated to live humbly with one another and serve others in love. As we serve through our spiritual gifts and love one another, we build up the whole body. God's Word is clear in this teaching.

From Him the whole body, joined and held together by every supporting ligament, grows and builds itself up in love, as each part does its work. (Ephesians 4:16)

Each one should use whatever gift he has received to serve others, faithfully administering grace in its various forms. (1 Peter 4:10)

For it is by grace you have been saved, though faith - and this not from yourselves, it is the gift of God - not by works, so that no one can boast. For we are God's workmanship, created in Christ Jesus to do good works, which God prepared in advance for us to do. (Ephesians 2: 8-10)

Fourth, mature disciples are trained for ministry, discovering and using their spiritual gifts, and finding their ministry passion. I have highlighted key phrases that point to the proper purpose for spiritual gifts.

It was he who gave some to be apostles, some to be prophets, some to be evangelists, and some to be pastors and teachers, *to prepare God's people for works of service*, so that *the body of Christ may be built up* until we all *reach unity* in the faith and *in the knowledge* of the Son of God and *become mature*, attaining to the whole measure of *the fullness of Christ*. (Ephesians 4:11-16).

CHAPTER 3   HOW TO BREATHE IN NEW LIFE

Following are some of my suggestions to pastors beginning a church revitalization process or who are currently in a very small church.   What may seem like common sense in the middle-sized church may not be reality in a struggling congregation. The list is not all encompassing, but it has been my approach to church revitalization.

I have learned that a pastor needs to use patient persuasion. Change should be introduced carefully after extensive listening and observation. I ask many questions about the congregation's history of highs and lows, former pastors, when the building was constructed, etc.   I also look for as many positives as I can point out in conversation. There are always a few people who doing most of the work, whether it's teaching Sunday School, mowing the grass, ushering, or doing unnoticed tasks behind the scene. When I discover who these workers are, I go out of my way to compliment them. I interview them. If I show appreciation for what is being done, they learn that I have not come to be a critical know-it-all. If I listen to folks, they will listen to me.

I firmly believe that all individuals are in need of being built-up, especially those who have kept the church operating. Perhaps it is my nature, but I like to verbalize appreciation by learning what they have done and then thanking them. When the pastor comes in like a breath of fresh air, and exhibits positive leadership with a big smile and a "can do" attitude, the workers are relieved because they feel like help has arrived.

1. Approach the declining church like a new church plant. Over the years, I have utilized the principles taught at seminars for church planters. By thinking like a church planter, the pastor will look more objectively at the church and consider what changes can be made. He will also think evangelistically and look for ways to reach out to the local community.

However, the revitalizing pastor has a few advantages that a church planter does not. The obvious one is that he is not starting from scratch. He already has a building, sanctuary seating, furniture, a core group, money in the bank, and some equipment. A disadvantage can be that the pastor will need to work within the current framework. Whatever foundation has been laid, it may need to be re-worked or replaced. I have found that long time members hang onto memories and want to keep their traditional operational paradigm. This is what they are familiar with and is in their comfort zone. This is why it is necessary to spend time with the influencers. If the pastor can get them to support a new vision, the rest of the congregation will come along.

2. Challenge small church thinking. Small churches often think they cannot have an impact on the community. The members are doing what they can to survive and have little vision for the future. They have no frame of reference other than what they know. The pastor must teach the church that they have something to offer. Begin by introducing the church's leaders to some church growth and evangelism books. I found it helpful to take them to seminars. The seminar speakers may inspire your people to consider new ideas. Create a discussion group that meets regularly to talk about what they have read or heard and encourage them to consider ways to reach out to the community. Help them to enlarge their vision by talking about the possibilities. Help them see the potential.

Small church thinking is usually illustrated by statements like: We have always done it that way. That will never work. Why would we want to change that? Hymns are what most people prefer to hear in church. It was good enough for my grandfather and it is good enough now.

Create a mission statement that the congregation can remember. I borrowed from an old church mission statement and changed it to fit my plan. I used the acronym, "B.B.T.S.& J." Bring them in (salvation), Build them up (recovery, discipleship), Train them for (ministry), and Send them out in Jesus' name (evangelism). This statement was mentioned so often that just about any member could quote it to you. It was printed everywhere. I even wrote a song that included the mission statement.

3. The pastor is the spark plug. The pastor can have an immediate impact with a "can-do" attitude. An enthusiastic pastor can set the tone. He must sell the church on the idea that God will do great things among them if they seek His direction. The pastor's role should be that of the coach and equipper for ministry. If he is seen as a figurehead, or even worse, just an employee rather than the leader, the congregation lacks biblical understanding. The pastor must carefully instruct the church on the biblical role of the pastor and have a personal goal of growing and developing as a leader and a manager of people.

A number of my peers subscribe to the philosophy that they should get to know the church before they suggest ideas and, therefore, should wait a year before enacting changes. I think this is a mistake because the congregation is more open to new ideas in the first year. The revitalizer is in an awkward situation where he must be diplomatic, but also be immediately active, not passive. Lyle Schaller addressed this perspective when he asks the question, "What should be the major emphasis during those first several months?"

> What is the best response of the new pastor to what appears to be a passive church? One piece of conventional wisdom suggests a comparatively passive and non-directive role during that first year. After studying scores of congregations that have recently completed their first year or two with a new minister, and after listening to thousands of laypersons from these same churches describe their reactions to that honeymoon year, the evidence strongly suggest that in the majority of cases the newly arrived minister should accept a more active leadership role.

4. Focus on evangelism and missions. The outward looking congregation considers local and foreign missions. Locally, too many churches are not in touch with their own community. People may drive through a neighborhood to reach their church without giving thought to the mission field surrounding it. They think evangelism is only about knocking on doors or handing out tracts. It is reaching out sincerely to their friends with the real love of God. I like the saying,

21

"We don't love people because we want to see them saved. We want to see them saved because we love them."

One of my favorite ways to create an evangelistic mindset is to send people out on short-term mission projects. The purpose is to encourage members to share their faith and to strengthen their walk with God. Usually the assignments are from one to four weeks. Money collected during Sunday School goes to support a short-term missions fund. Friends are also willing to contribute to the fund because they know the people who are planning to go. The goal is for the church to pay for the entire cost of short term trips (including airfare) so that the members do not need to raise money. Rarely was there a lack of money to send anyone anywhere.

Short-term missions has a powerful impact on the individual who has never been to another country. For some, it is the first time they have been on an airplane. I have seen tentative people return with more confidence and a life-changing story to tell. I know of one team in particular that experienced such camaraderie that after ten years they were still talking about it.

Over the years, we sent individuals, couples, and small teams around the world. There was only one criterion for going. Those who went were expected to give a presentation on Sunday morning. In fact, the presentation was in lieu of the sermon. I learned that returnees were excited and had plenty to say. The presentation included stories, photos, lots of laughter, and some time for questions from the audience. These presentations went a long way toward inspiring others to go as well.

Usually teams went through a denominational missions program or with a para-church organization. Many went to work in the deaf schools in Jamaica or helped build church facilities. Other destinations included Albania, Alaska, Argentina, Armenia, California, Columbia, India, Kentucky, New York City, Virginia, and college campus organizations.

We have a Biblical mandate from Jesus himself in Matthew 28:18-20, "All authority in heaven and on earth has been given to me. Therefore, go and make disciples of all nations, baptizing them in the name of the Father and of the Son and of the Holy Spirit, and teaching them to obey everything I have commanded you. And surely I am with you always, to the very end of the age."

5. Who is your audience? You are likely to attract the same type of people you already have in your congregation. Who fits best into your church? What kinds of people will probably return after their first visit? Like ice cream, there are all kinds of church flavors. Regarding our audience, Rick Warren gives some wise advice,

> Don't try to be something you're not. If your church is primarily made up of elderly folks, decide to become the most effective ministry to senior citizens that you can possibly be. Don't try to become a baby-buster congregation. Strengthen what you are already doing and don't worry about what you can't do. Keep doing what you've been strong at, just do it better. Chances are that there's a pocket of people in your community that only your church can reach.

I recognize that my style of ministry isn't for everybody. If a church's mission is to reach out to college students, then the church will have a different dynamic than one geared toward multigenerational families. Your music style will reflect the congregation's dominant preference. I dress up according to the venue where I am speaking. If I have a blue jeans and t-shirt kind of church, I don't wear my suit. As it has been said, "It takes all kinds of churches to reach all kinds of people."

6. Make financial adjustments. This may entail sending less money to the denomination's national office. The congregation needs all the money it has for revitalization. Use the money to pay staff, advertise, buy training materials, and make whatever upgrades needed. Usually small congregations think they have to show up in the yearly denominational report in order to prove they are a viable church. The truth is that the church rarely gets back its "investment" and is better served by investing in its own development. If a representative calls asking for money, just tell them that you are concentrating on home missions. Instead of the church asking the national office for financial assistance, I think you ought to send in half of the recommended amount to the denomination.

When I arrived at my first church, it had shrunk to seventeen people and was behind on the mortgage. Although the church only owed $15,000 on the property, they had not made the mortgage payment for a number of months. Fortunately, the loan was with our denomination. I called the loan officer and arranged to stop the interest on the loan so the church could focus on paying the principle. The representative was very cooperative and accepted my offer, as long as we did not miss any more payments. The church was ecstatic and immediately discussed ways to pay off the mortgage. A group of hard working women dedicated themselves to hand stitching quilt tops for people in the area and applied all the proceeds toward the loan. The church was debt free within three years.

The pastor is doing the denomination a favor by helping the church become self-sufficient and not dependent on subsidies. When my second church grew past one hundred in attendance, a denominational representative noticed that we had not increased our contribution and asked what the church was doing with its money. I said, "They are paying the bills, investing in the church's ministries, and paying the preacher". He laughed and thanked me for my honesty.

I am not saying that the pastor should exhibit a negative attitude toward the national office. Of course the congregation should send support to the denomination. I think the pastor can explain his strategy without creating any misunderstanding. Eventually, as the congregation grows it should increase its portion.

7. Give the church new vision. When coming into an established congregation, the new pastor must have a game plan; an idea of what God wants him to do. This is not easy, especially for a young pastor who is relating to adults much older than himself. I cannot emphasize enough the importance of showing respect toward the influential leaders. For whatever reason, they are in a place of influence and decision-making.

Immediately, the pastor should discern who the influencers are in the church and listen to them. Find out what gets them excited.

Discover what matters to them. Take them out to breakfast and sit across the table and interview them. They will usually appreciate that someone cared enough to ask their opinion. By spending time with the influencers, the pastor will learn the history of the church and why things operate the way they do. When people have been heard they are more willing to listen to the pastor's proposals for change.

There are a series of related questions to be asked of each individual: What kind of church would you like to see us become? What suggestions do you have for making our church even better than it is? What would you like to see happen at our church that has never happened before? If you could do anything at our church, what would it be? The purpose in asking these types of questions is to start "possibility thinking". The pastor is the visionary, but the vision is also a group dynamic. If the congregation can see that God wants to do something special in their church, vision has been communicated.

At the church board meetings, I always introduced an idea by saying, "I want to ask your opinion on something. I would like us to consider doing so and so. What are your thoughts?" Often, the feedback was positive and the church representatives appreciated that I was asking for their input. This approach goes a long way toward building a working relationship. Going into a church and acting like a dictator is counter productive. When the congregational decision makers own the idea, the rest of the church body will usually come along.

8. Try to phase out outdated activities. What is the purpose of a "homecoming"? For some rural churches, it is the only time of the year when the sanctuary is full. It is an opportunity to see people who no longer attend the church and to talk about the good old days. I am not belittling homecomings. But, does this mean that the best days of the church are behind them? Newer attendees are not acquainted with people who used to come to the church. The obvious question is, "Why aren't they coming now?" Instead of focusing on the past, look to the future. The church's history is important. However, unless it is only a frame of reference, it doesn't work toward the future.

Lyle Schaller, a writer who did extensive research on small churches, noted that younger and newer leadership does not dwell on the past. "In general terms, the younger the members, and especially the leaders, the stronger the future orientation, the greater the willingness to take risks and the higher the turnover rate within the membership. The older the members, the greater the probability there will be an interest in recreating yesterday."

There may be traditions that are continued because the church has an emotional attachment to them, but which have very little value. Why not introduce new traditions that are outward looking? Start yearly events that welcome new people: Friend Day, church picnic, music festival, fall potluck, Christmas play, Halloween alternative, and anything that is fun for children. But keep in mind the old saying, "Don't tear down the fence until you know why it was built." Respect what the church has done in the past that worked well. If there is an outdated event that people want to keep, ask if there are ways it can be improved.

In our congregation, the Wednesday night service was a tradition that had run its course. No more than six people regularly attended. Because there was so little interest, I asked the Church Board if it was okay to discontinue the midweek service. I saw an opportunity to introduce cell groups in lieu of the midweek service. The Board members were in favor of the change, especially since I suggested a replacement. I announced the formation of a cell group immediately. I was elated when twenty-five people came to the first meeting. Within the year, we had three functioning home groups.

9. Encourage hospitality. The gift of hospitality is one of the most powerful ministry gifts in the Body of Christ. There are people who love to host. They are great at putting together dinner parties. Inviting people to a home cookout goes a long way toward assimilation. I have a friend who is terrific at putting on a party at her home and introducing the "new berries" to the "old berries".

People are lonely. If they have a full time job, they probably lack fellowship outside the work place. Find ways to connect people and build friendships. Small home groups are an excellent way for new people to get to know others. The more entryways into your fellowship the better. Fellowship activities like men's basketball, fishing trips, steak cookouts, service projects, and sightseeing tours give people an opportunity to make new friends. Many people will go to a church function when they are invited by a friend. Most of us are shy and appreciate when someone introduces us to their friends. Fun fellowship activities are a way to introduce one's friend to long time members in a non-threatening way.

10. "Big Event" activities are something that can rally the congregation. Each year a church can budget for events like Easter, Christmas, Harvest Party, Mother and Father's Day, and other crowd gathering activities. Our Valentine Banquet grew every year to become extremely popular. There were occasions when we could not find a restaurant large enough to fit our needs. This event was well organized. For entertainment, a lot of preparation went into silly skits and humorous songs put on by the parishioners, and occasionally an invited speaker. The room was beautifully decorated and the guests were assigned to tables with flower arrangements, treats and small gifts. Everyone received a door prize when the banquet was over. There are a number of reasons to have "Big Events":

Big Events build morale by giving a winning team feeling.

They don't drain the congregation's resources.

It makes noise in the community and says that something is happening.

The congregation is encouraged by a large crowd.

The events can help stretch the congregation's faith and goal setting.

It gives opportunities for members to invite their unchurched friends.

The congregation can point to an accomplishment.

It unites people and increases the pool of volunteers.

11. Have fun serving the Lord and others will, too. People like joy and enthusiasm. They are attracted to a positive environment. An old saying says, "To be enthusiastic you must act enthusiastic." Too many churches do not have fun and celebration in their worship services. Be excited about your ministry and others will be, too. I think the pastor can have fun without embarrassing the congregation. I encourage people to laugh with me when I tell a humorous story. Seekers often comment on how they enjoyed coming to church.

The pastor can set the tone on Sunday mornings. At one church, the pastor who preceded me insisted that the congregation be "quiet and respectful" in the sanctuary, so no one spoke while waiting for the service to begin. I saw this when I visited before I became the pastor. The atmosphere was depressing, boring, and joyless. Why would anyone want to go to such a church? On my first Sunday as pastor, I enthusiastically entered the sanctuary - not overly loud or obnoxious, but with a presence that communicated, "I am glad to be here!" I wanted to create an air of anticipation. It wasn't long before people started laughing and greeting each other.

I enjoy showing a movie clip that is funny and sets up the sermon. When I opened a series on the subject of prayer, I played a scene from the comedy, "Sister Act". It's the scene where Whoopi Goldberg is asked to pray before dinner. It's hilarious as she nervously stumbles through the prayer using parts of poems and songs. What an intro! When the audience stopped laughing, I asked, "Have you ever found yourself in that sort of situation? I know I have. In the next few weeks we are going to talk about talking to God." Humor draws people's attention and helps them to focus.

12. Survey the congregation. By surveying the congregation, a new pastor discovers the things that matter to his parishioners. A survey can inform the pastor about the cultural makeup of the congregation. What kind of music is the dominate style? What events or fellowship activities would they like to have? What would they like to see happen in their church? When are they the most busy? What suggestions do they have? By doing a survey, the pastor may learn what changes he can introduce. The purpose of the survey is not to focus inwardly, but to get an idea of how the church thinks. Are they evangelistic? What community concerns do they have? What kind of change are they open to?

I found that the survey was a way of demonstrating my interest in people's opinions. I recommend a survey soon after the pastor arrives. Jim Herrington recommends the survey as a good assessment tool.

> A surprising large number of church leaders avoid feedback. They seem to have no interest in getting an accurate reading on the congregation's pulse. A comprehensive assessment tool can provide a broad indication of the perception of the membership. A survey highlights the areas of relative strength, or health, and the areas that currently need the most attention. Periodic surveys can show important trends for consideration in the ongoing design of the change process.

A survey also helps to determine what kind of music style is the most popular in the church. Ask them about the radio stations they listen to and about their favorite artists or bands. For instance, if Country music is the most popular then find ways to incorporate Southern Gospel music into the worship service. If you have a church made up of college students, Contemporary Christian is probably the style they prefer.

13. Market your church. Make noise in your community. Name recognition is vital when attracting newcomers who have moved to the community. Sponsor events that attract attention and are newsworthy. Small town newspapers especially want stories to fill the religion section. We submitted articles whenever we were going to have a public event. Some congregations place ads in the newspaper and purchase radio time. We had considerable success with television ads and mass mailing to the community.

We bought the rights to seven television commercials. These were professional 30-second spots with a voice-over and a printed tag at the end with our website address. These were highly successful. We saw an increase in the number of hits to our website.

Every church should have a website. It takes time to develop one but it is a wonderful way to communicate to people who are looking for a church. On our website, we included information about fellowship activities, youth ministries, ministry opportunities, a map to the church, photographs, the ministry staff, our core beliefs, and other information people usually ask about. It is important that the church website is up to date. Is the phone number out of order? Is the map clear with easy to follow directions? Is there contact information? Can visitors learn what your beliefs are? Try to anticipate what questions people may have. It is a good idea to have someone evaluate the website and make suggestions.

Use all the new internet avenues available. Make use of Twitter, Facebook, blogs, email, and whatever new comes along. If you have someone who keeps up with the latest software and social sites, put them to work.

Our Strategic Team was always looking for new ways to get our name out. We rented a county fair booth that was highly successful. Above the booth was a large professionally made banner with our website address. In the booth was a TV showing recordings of our children's ministry. We also had a display of 8×10 group photos, a list of our ministries, and brochures with a map. We gave away helium-filled balloons with the church's name printed on them and Tootsie Roll Pops were tied to the string of each balloon. A large bowl of candy was placed in front of the display. We had plenty of volunteers working in shifts.

Christmas and Independence Day Parades are easy and fun. Families love to participate by decorating and riding on the float. Every 4th of July one of the towns held an annual celebration at the town park. Each year we set up a booth, a large banner, and gave away free watermelon and bottled water. On our table, we had a stack of our brochures.

I created the "Reach Out Newsletter". Articles were written by people who attended the church and covered a theme that would relate to the unchurched. It was an effective tool in the community. Our goal was to "reach out" to our sphere of influence. We eventually mailed to about 12,000 households quarterly. That number of households covers a large area in a rural setting. It was a good way to market the church and create "buzz" in the community. Name recognition is a long-range venture that pays off for years to come. When our members mentioned what church they attended, people had a positive view of the church and usually said that they have heard of it. Our goal was to be on the "let's visit that church" list.

Realize that church marketing is never meant to be an end in itself, but a means to an end. The end, of course, is the delivery of truth and love, in Christ's name and for God's glory, to our gospel-resistant culture. Without compromising one iota of the gospel, we are challenged to serve God by cultivating our ministry fields for a full spiritual harvest. Marketing is simply one of the tools we can employ to maximize the harvest that God has prepared.

14. Befriend the doorkeepers. I recall one evening service when I was discouraged that the head trustee was the only one to show up. I had only been at the church for a month and recognized that I had an opportunity to chat privately with him. He was a quiet retired man who cared deeply about the facilities. I asked him to show me around. He seemed surprised that I wanted a tour. For two hours he told me about his concerns. At the end he said something that I won't forget, "Ya know, I have never had anybody ask for my opinion or want to know what needs to be fixed." Not long after that conversation, he donated a large sum of money to expand the parking lot. He told me later that after talking to me he knew we would need more room for parking.

The pastor entering a church with a history of non-growth will need to be able to communicate new ideas. He should be respectful of the "leadership" in place - the influential matriarchs and patriarchs, and long-term core people. The pastor must have good relational skills because relationships are important in any church. Carl F. George advises the pastor to focus on the opinion makers.

> Opinion makers in your church or ministry are natural leaders who will influence people whether or not you give them formal positions in your organization. Without their support, any ministry's goal implementation will be shaky at best. This is especially critical in the small church.

Usually the influencers will give you permission to make changes if you include them in the process. I think they become defensive when the pastor forgets to seek their opinion and does not listen to their concerns. Change can be threatening to those who are used to traditional forms. Listening helps you earn the right to be heard.

15. Teach the tradition of change. What if the pastor taught that the new "tradition" is the tradition of change? In other words, explain that the church can be led by the Holy Spirit to new ideas if the church spends time in prayer regarding God's direction. Ask the opinion makers what they think God wants the church to do. The goal is perpetual improvement. Not change for change's sake, nor dropping programs on a whim, but being open to God's work in their midst.

Christians who move into the area have "fresh eyes". Usually, they begin to talk about ministries that their larger home church does, "At our old church we did such and such. Do you think that is something we could do here?" Some suggestions are easily transferable. I am encouraged when a new, well-liked attendee suggests something that I have wanted to do. Old members tend to be more open to new ideas coming from them, especially if the person offers to head up a new ministry.

16. Renovate the facilities. Everything in my second church had been donated: worn hymnbooks, carved up pews, orange-yellow carpet, the upright piano, old hand made tables, and the building was located next to an interstate highway with no air conditioning and open windows in the summertime. It took time, but we gradually replaced many of these items, giving our facility a fresh look.

What is a visitor's first impression of your church's building when they drive into the parking lot? The church's facilities can telegraph a positive image to visitors and to the community. Fix and upgrade parking signs, add landscaping, expand the parking lot, paint the sanctuary, redecorate the women's restroom and perk up the nursery. It does not cost anything to pick up all the trash near your building. Even though a small church has financial limitations, paint can do wonders. Improvements create an atmosphere of excitement and freshness. Have your leadership people walk with you toward the building entrance and walk around the grounds. Ask them to look at the facilities from the view of a visitor and observe what improvements can be made. There is something about making physical improvements that can jump-start morale.

Now, what I am about to say is really going to bother some congregational leaders. The truth is – in order to survive, a congregation may need to move to a more visible location. Your building may be beautiful, historic, and up to date. But, if it's off the beaten path, only a few will know that your church exists. Out of sight, out of mind. The difference between an older church and a new church plant is that the new church will meet where it can easily be found by visitors. Where do you usually find a McDonalds? In the most visible location possible. It helps to be near a well-traveled street.

17. Put up directional signs. There is nothing more disconcerting than not being able to find your way around. A visitor should be able to locate the restroom, nursery, classrooms, and office by just glancing around. Some church buildings are like mazes. I have been in buildings where I could not find the sanctuary! Some churches have maps at an "information booth". Print brochures informing newcomers about your various ministry programs and their locations on a map. Directional signs also communicate organization and a hospitable atmosphere.

A weakness for many rural congregations is their poor location. Frequently, they are not near a main highway and are hard to find. If the church is not willing to move to another location for visibility, then the church must invest in road signs. When new people move into the area, they only see the noticeable buildings and visit those churches first. There are ways around this problem. Directions can be placed on the church website, in a community newsletter, in newspaper ads, blogs, or even on business cards.

18. Preach for spiritual revival. Pastors make a mistake when they assume everyone in their congregation is a devoted follower of Christ. Often the ungodly attitudes exhibited by the influencers are the result of an un-surrendered life. They live according to the sinful nature. They are "me" centered rather than Christ centered. If the church is not growing, it might be related to a weak commitment to

Jesus and the Gospel. In order for a congregation to discover God's plan for their church, they need to have a personal encounter with God. How can we expect the members to evangelize the world when they themselves have grown cold and are in need of personal revival? They cannot reproduce what they are not.

In Galatians 5:19-21, the Apostle Paul addresses the symptoms associated with an unrepentant heart. "The acts of the sinful nature are obvious: sexual immorality, impurity and debauchery, idolatry and witchcraft, hatred, discord, jealousy, fits of rage, selfish ambition, dissensions, factions and envy, drunkenness, orgies, and the like. I warn you, as I did before, that those who live like this will not inherit the kingdom of God."

The purpose of preaching is to effectively encounter the sinfulness of the human situation with the intention of affecting the heart of individuals in such a way that they understand that without Christ they are eternally lost and guilty of sin. Preaching challenges people to repent. Preaching centered in Christ is confrontational because people are brought to a place of decision.

I am reminded of the Methodist circuit riders who preached during the Second Great Awakening in the United States. These preachers were known for their heartfelt sermons. These itinerant preachers were very different from the college-educated ministers of their day. They rarely read their sermons, as the Anglicans or Congregationalists did, but instead exhorted the people passionately from the Bible, using anecdotes, illustrations, and analogies from everyday life. They learned how to preach passionately by listening to passionate preaching. Yet it was not their oratory that won their audiences. It was their power.

Preaching is a way to wake up the sleeping church. If I were to go into a dying church, I would pray for revival to sweep the congregation. I would encourage the congregation to bring their own Bible and follow along as I preach and teach. I would preach with Holy Spirit expectancy and anointed power. What happens when God moves and revival breaks out? God brings a wave of conviction of sin and the need for repentance. By leading people to Jesus Christ and developing His disciples, we are expanding the Kingdom of God. God is going to bless anyone who follows Christ's instructions to His church.

I highly recommend that the adult Sunday School class or classes read the book, *The Calvary Road*, by Roy Hession. This small Christian classic can have an impact on the attitude of the older members in the church. It helps the reader to examine his walk with God and his attitudes toward others. I have introduced this book in Sunday School classes. It cuts to the chase and it's convicting. When believers are close to God, the fellowship is sweet and joyous. If they love Jesus, the love of God will naturally flow out to those around them.

Good preaching is a factor in turning a church around and sustaining its growth. Dynamic preachers have a positive impact on the Sunday morning service, especially upon visitors. Expository preaching also has been suggested as beneficial to church growth. Biblical teaching reinforces God's purpose for the church as the pastor boldly encourages members to play their part in the ministry to which God has called them. Thom Rainer asserts that preaching is crucial,

> Few on our research team were surprised that preaching and church growth are related, particularly preaching and conversion growth. The surprise was in the intensity and quality of the responses. Among all the possible factors that led a church to evangelistic growth, preaching was clearly the most important element. Over 90 percent of the respondents indicated preaching was a major factor in their churches' evangelistic effectiveness.

Preach and teach that everyone can have a personal relationship with Jesus Christ. Growing churches are not ashamed of the Gospel because that is their main objective. If pastors are not preaching the Word of God - all the other items listed here are man-made and worthless. The true measure of successful ministry is whether or not people are coming to faith in Christ. Are lives being changed because of your Christ-centered focus? I use the New International Version because it is easier for the average person to understand. I choose not to participate in a translation debate - just read the Bible translation you like best!

19. Work at becoming visitor-friendly. I have visited churches that didn't acknowledge that my wife and I were in the building. We have had greeters who handed us a bulletin and not looked our way. That is not the way to make a good impression! It reminds me of when a teenager goes to a dance and no one speaks to them, much less ask them to dance. Have you ever gone to a banquet and not know where to sit, or to a party where you were left standing in the corner? We have had this experience in both large and small churches.

It's scary to visit a church and feel out of place. "Where is the restroom?" or "Where's the nursery?" Can a visitor find the location of rooms without asking? Are the ushers and greeters doing their job? Are visitors given a bulletin and welcomed? Is the bulletin easy to read and informative? Is the service user-friendly and easy to follow? Does the service flow, or are there too many "dead air" times? Do the members of the congregation introduce themselves? Have a "meet and greet" time after the initial praise and worship phase. Someone on the worship team can say, "Turn to somebody and say, "I'm glad you're here!" After about five minutes, an upbeat "gathering song" can be used to cue people to return to their seats. This is an easy way for members to speak to the visitors.

It is not a good idea to ask visitors to stand and introduce themselves. If they are shopping around for a church, they may want to remain anonymous. They are visiting area churches and are just "kicking the tires." This subject is somewhat subjective depending one's individual experiences and culture. I think it is best to let the visitor remain anonymous. A nice smile and a warm welcome is all that is necessary.

20. Improve the quality of the bulletin. Collect bulletins from other churches until you find a style that you would like to duplicate. By collecting bulletins, you can get some good ministry ideas and see how your church is progressing. Be encouraged - there are many terrible bulletins out there that look worse then yours! After I had collected around fifty, I studied them for layout ideas, printing, clip-art, wording, paper stock, paper size, and kept the best ones on hand. Look out for "Christianese", denomination acronyms, clutter, dumb humor, inside jokes, or anything that keeps the bulletin from being "visitor friendly". Print announcements using first and last names so that new people can learn names. By printing the entire name, you are not assuming that everyone knows who Tom is. It is recommended that the writing be on an eighth grade reading level. Ask several friends outside your church to review your bulletin and give you some suggestions, especially regarding items that may be confusing.

With today's computer software a church can design a bulletin cover at home that is unique. Besides, it is also a way to save money. I went to a printer and had 5000 copies made of several covers that we designed.

Do not put the attendance in the bulletin. People tend to exaggerate how many attend their church when talking to friends! Do not let people judge your church because of its size. Highlight every activity you can think of in order to fill up any space. A full bulletin gives the appearance that a lot is going on.

21. Improve the worship music. This can be difficult because the smaller church often has few musicians. Do whatever you can to improve the music. Find the style that relates best to your audience and invest in its success. If the church needs a piano - find one. If the sound system needs to be replaced - replace it. If you need a piano player - pray for a good one! I remember when our church sang mostly hymns without a piano player. We prayed and God sent us a pianist. Eventually, we had too many piano players, guitar players, and other musicians, so we formed three worship teams. God wanted us to worship! We purchased whatever the worship teams needed including: a bass guitar, a drum set, additional microphones and stands, instrument cords, amps, and a subscription to an internet music library.

Avoid depressing songs. Many congregations are using both traditional and contemporary music in the same worship service. Whatever style the congregation prefers, work on the quality of musicianship as much as possible. I heard Rick Warren say that the music is almost as important as the sermon, and that a church is known by the style of music it plays on Sunday morning. I think younger visitors expect upbeat music. Good musicians attract other good musicians.

It is a blessing to have a hymn leader with a charismatic personality who can lead a song enthusiastically. A problem can occur when a song leader chooses hymns that do not flow and the congregation does not know. I have had people choose "funeral dirges" that were depressing to sing. Then, there are those song directors who insist on giving the historic background of each hymn. One woman bragged about the new song in the hymnbook that was written in the 1950s! We have incorporated hymns in with the praise and worship music. A real plus has been the influx of re-arranged hymns. This has helped hymns become mufti-generational.

It is my observation that non-traditional music is the growing trend in churches today. I prefer praise and worship because I want to reach out to a younger audience. I assume they prefer upbeat music, whether it be rock and roll or "new" country music. Studies have shown that growing churches are less likely to use traditional music in Sunday morning worship. Non-traditional churches have a significantly higher percentage of attendees compared to members of predominately traditional churches.

22. Find cheerful greeters and ushers. What a terrible thing to meet an unhappy greeter! You may want to appoint the nicest people you can find to greet regularly. They can set a good example for new greeters. I like greeters who look at me, give a warm handshake, and exhibit a welcoming countenance. We had a widow who was middle-aged, kind, and had a sweet persona. Doris had never served in this capacity before. Needless to say, she was nervous at first. Nevertheless, this wonderful woman became great at her job. When she wasn't at church, people wondered if she was okay. Doris trained other greeters and served as our chief greeter for over ten years.

As John Maxwell is fond of saying, "We need ushers who ush!" Ushers are assistants, guides and servants. Train them to be polite and positive. Find those individuals who are naturals at meeting people.

They are the visitor's first impression of the congregation. Have them wear name tags to identify themselves. We prefer that the same people act as ushers so that they become comfortable with meeting new people. Talented greeters and ushers know who the visitors are and can help you with names. A good usher will look for open seats and escort visitors and families so that they will not stand around wondering where they should sit. Ushers should have a servant's attitude.

23. Have membership mean something. Raise the expectation bar. Peter Wagner says that churches need to increase commitment by doing two things, "raise your requirements for new members and raise the commitment level for current members." Wagner goes into detail about the membership requirements at Calvary Community Church in Thousand Oaks, California and lists the requirements for becoming a member:

> Signing your name to a covenant.
>
> Attending weekly worship.
>
> Spending one night per week with the family in planned family activities.
>
> Participating in a small group that meets weekly.
>
> Committing yourself to regular, substantial giving to the church.
>
> Locating a ministry in the church in which you can use your spiritual gifts.
>
> Promising to spend time each day in personal devotions.

Many churches inflate statistics by keeping an "inactive" membership list. They have five hundred members on their rolls and only seventy-five people in the worship service. What is an "inactive member" but someone who no longer wants to attend? It takes too much effort to chase after those who decided long ago to stop coming.

With a few exceptions, chasing after past members is a waste of time. It usually takes about five times more energy to reactivate a disgruntled or carnal member than it does to win a receptive unbeliever. I believe God has called pastors to catch fish and feed sheep, not corral goats! Your inactive members probably need to join somewhere else for a number of reasons. If you want to grow, focus on reaching receptive people.

24. Encourage celebration. It is okay to clap when someone has a good report. Celebrate graduations, anniversaries, and all other milestones. Whether on Sunday morning or in a small group setting, the church is wise to celebrate as a community. As Rick Warren notes, "At Saddleback, we've found that people are more receptive to the Gospel when they face changes like a new marriage, a new baby, a new home, a new job, or a new school."

There are many opportunities to celebrate. I remember when a young husband announced that he and his wife were going to have triplets. The church erupted with applause. Whenever one of our short-term mission teams gave a presentation we celebrated what they had done with cheers and clapping. Another time, when a young dating couple announced their engagement, the congregation cheered and gave a standing ovation.

In the morning worship service, acknowledge and celebrate all volunteers. Literally celebrate a volunteer every Sunday. Build them up! Tell the congregation what the volunteer does and why they are special. I cannot emphasize enough the need to celebrate and be grateful for the work people do. When people are celebrated, a positive environment develops.

25. Build male leadership. No church can function without the devoted, godly women who stay at the church through thick and thin. Women are the smaller church's backbone, but men give it strength. The goal is to have a balance of men and women involved in the congregational decision-making.

Men who visit a church may notice that women dominate church life, thereby giving the impression that the congregation is "feminized". For this reason, I look for ways to involve men in the worship service. Their presence sends a signal to visiting husbands that going to church is okay. Just because men attend church does not mean they are wimps. Have men take up the offering, make announcements, play on the worship team, hand out bulletins or be a floating greeter.

It is a blessing to have a successful men's group. The main key is to find a leader that men like and respect. Our men worked at developing a men's fellowship that was fun and inclusive. By and large, I think men are lonely. Anything that helps men make new friends works well. When the guys met and discussed what their friends outside the church would be interested in, they started planning. They realized that the activities they wanted to do were the same as their friends. I did what I could to encourage their brainstorming and "released" them to take action. They organized a salt water fishing trip, a movie and dinner at a restaurant that served "man" food, a monthly men's breakfast at the church that featured sausage gravy and biscuits, they took trips to Civil War sites, held Bible studies in their homes, started installing new roofs on the homes of the poor, did fund raising by selling barbequed chicken, and went on father/son outings. As a result, the men's group doubled in size. When men start attending the church their families usually attend, too.

I am not suggesting that women turn over the church to the men. That is ridiculous. In my opinion, the most talented people are women! Women tend to be more spiritually connected than men are. In fact, they worry about their husbands and pray that they will go to church with them. I am reminded of a sign I read in an office that said, "Do you want to talk to the man in charge, or to the woman who knows everything?"

26. Kids beget kids and kids beget parents. The yearly budget ought to reflect what matters the most to the church. Promote youth ministry. It is the most important ministry in the church. It is too often devalued and under budgeted. When a church emphasizes youth ministry, from nursery to college age, word gets out in the community. Especially in a low demographic area where there may be few opportunities for children's activities.

Parents will do anything for their children. When parents are looking for a church, they usually want to know if there are children. George Barna says that the youth ministry is the most important

41

ministry in the church because moral foundations are set by age nine. Parents are looking for quality ministry for their children. The youth ministry is the most important program within the church for several reasons:

> Children bring parents to church and parents are looking for a church that has other children.

> Children are noisy and noise is a sign of activity.

> Children allow adults to practice their ministry skills through Sunday School, nursery or Vacation Bible School.

> When children come to church, they are open to the gospel and more likely to receive Christ.

> Some parents who only come to church to give their children a "moral education" become followers of Jesus themselves.

> Children cause the congregation's demographics to become younger.

> Kids are cute and are a lot of fun. Other family members will come to see a child in a play or program.

In my last church, the youth ministry exploded with kids. Our programs grew and changed according to the fluctuation in ages we had over the years. In my last church the attendance grew from thirty-five to two hundred - about a dozen of the original thirty-five were children.

When I arrived, I began emphasizing youth ministry and made it the primary ministry focus of the church. For years, there had been no consistent youth program. I decided that in order for the church to grow I needed to attract young families and knew that activities for youth were important to them. The fun part of youth ministry is the opportunity to be creative and experiment with new activities.

Here are a few ideas. We did the usual programs found in most churches. We also added a puppet theater were the middle school students made their own puppets, stage, and wrote their own scripts. Vacation Bible School included pony rides, clowns, live music, outdoor crafts, moon bounce, games and the like. We changed the VBS venue to a park some years.

A program that was very successful was M.A.P. (Mentor Advocate Program) - High school and middle school students are paired with an adult advocate who meets with their young person regularly. In order to become an advocate, a person must be a devoted Christian and a church member. The advocate contacts their teenager once a week in order to build a mentoring relationship. Similar to Big Brother and Big Sisters. Students chose their advocate.

Our Lock-ins drew many high school kids. We rented an entire community center. A low turn out was fifty. One year we had hundred-fifty. Usually, over half were unchurched. We played large group games such as one would find at a Youth for Christ or Young Life Conference. If available, we arranged to have Christian bands from the local college. The Gospel was shared later in the evenings.

Another yearly activity was the Family Fun Fair. This was held in the spring on the church grounds. All food including cotton candy, popcorn, hotdogs, ice cream, and candy was free. The games were geared toward elementary school ages and manned by the high school students. We rented an inflatable moon bounce, dunking booth, and other game equipment. Helium balloons with the church logo were given to all children. The purpose for the investment was simple: easy marketing, a free event for young families, introduced our church to the unchurched or those looking for a church, involved up to fifty volunteers, and established our church as a place to visit. We always had a large number of Sunday morning visitors after the fair.

27. Equip for ministry. One weakness in any church is the lack of leaders. I discovered that when more people are involved in the church, more is done. Many hands make light work. Because the pool of leaders is so small in the struggling church, the pastor can end up doing everything.

Develop a training program in your church. Start your own "how-to" classes that teach practical ministry application. Over the years I taught classes on leading a small group, preparing a Bible study, organizing an event, having a quiet time, managing your finances, leading worship, hospital visitation etiquette, leading a youth ministry, friendship evangelism, friendship counseling, world religions, and leadership training. Budget money for sending people to seminars to receive specific training. We utilized programs like Consumer Credit Counseling, the Billy Graham School of Evangelism, John Maxwell Lay Leadership seminars, Youth Sponsor retreats, Worship Leaders seminars, and Small Group Leadership seminars. We also sponsored a Walk Thru the Bible event that was open to the public. Almost all of the adults in our church attended.

The key is to let others participate in relevant ministry. Let them learn on the job and allow for mistakes. Release the church! Creating an environment that will attract leaders is vital to any organization. That is the job of a leader. They must be active; they must generate activity that is productive; and they must encourage, create, and facilitate changes in the organization. They must create a climate in which potential leaders will thrive. John Maxwell says that the leader's toughest challenge is to create an atmosphere that attracts new leaders.

28. Always evaluate your ministry. After attending a John Maxwell seminar, I decided to organize a Strategic Planning Team. My purpose was to meet with people who were interested in the quality of our ministry. Each time we met, I asked the following questions: How's business? Not, how many do we have in attendance - but what are we doing to honor Christ? This is our church: What is meaningful to us? How can we improve? What does God want us to do next? Does it work? Everyone is welcome join in the discussion.

The goal has always been to evaluate and improve what we are doing and to brainstorm. I have taught that change is good and that there is no such thing as a small church. If Jesus is in our midst, anything can happen. Whether one is revitalizing a church or moving a church to the next level, the need for evaluation still applies.

We prayed for God's guidance. What is God calling us to next? What is the next chapter in our congregational life history supposed to look like, and how do we get there? These questions are at the foundation of a new dream or a different vision. And the new dream carries with it the energy and the direction to start a new cycle in the history of the congregation with new enthusiasms and commitments. The joke around the church is – don't get too comfortable with what we're doing now because next year it is going to be different!

29. Search for creative ideas. Creativity is an ongoing process, and there are times when you have no fresh ideas. Attend seminars and learn from those who are doing what they teach. There is no need to reinvent the wheel. If somebody has a good idea - use it. Ask your members to bring bulletins from other churches when they are away.

Some of the best ideas come from people who are new to your church. They have "fresh eyes" and see things that you do not. There are changes that they could recommend. Often, new people have come from other congregations with particular ministries that they did well. In fact, when new people start making suggestions, it may be because they had participated in a ministry in their former church. Their suggestions ought to be considered.

Creativity keeps the congregation on the cutting "edge" and helps avoid complacency. Ed Young, who is the pastor of one of the fastest growing churches in the United States, talks a lot about creativity.

During the ten years of Fellowship Church's life, we have learned that creativity is pivotal to building an exciting church that will make a difference in people's lives. Creativity brings people in the front door, and creativity keeps people from going out the back door. It doesn't matter the size of the church, its makeup, its budget, or the demographics: Creativity can be applied to all situations. Creativity is linked to change.

30. Protect the congregation. The church must be a safe place for the wounded. The leaders must circle the wagons when there is an antagonist/wolf in the church. The pastor/shepherd should not apologize when he drives wolves away and protects the sheep. Psalm 22:10 states, *"Drive out the mocker, and out goes strife; quarrels and insults are ended."* Remove people who have a history of hurting others in the congregation or who are bent on promoting heresy.

One way to protect the congregation from antagonistic people who move from church to church is to raise membership requirements.

45

Specifically, require that a new person must regularly attend for at least six months in order to become a member. This practice goes against the "seeker church" approach, but it should be considered by pastors who have experienced a procession of difficult people passing through the church.

The truth is that the pastor might be the one who needs to be protected from the wolves. Difficult people can rob a pastor's joy. I always appreciated parishioners who defended me from unfair criticism or character assassins. There are those who think their job is to "keep the pastor in line."

(See the Chapter on Antagonists.)

31. Take care of the pastor's family. Relationships at home are most important. The call to minister comes first on the home front. It is out of this perspective of putting family first in ministry that the importance of the church family and the church as family arises. Protect your family from criticism and from unfair expectations. Your spouse and children are not for sale, for hire, or for belittling. The pastor should never tell stories that could embarrass his family.

The pastor should not feel guilty for taking a vacation with his family. He needs to rest. I always felt like I had to stay on the job. I thought that I wasn't being true to my calling if I took a break. Time away is good for your family and your church. Take the opportunity to visit another church or go on a spiritual retreat. The longer the break, the better. Some pastors are able to take off for an entire summer month. By the way, please turn off all the communication devices.

32. Don't compare your church with larger churches. City churches and rural churches have different dynamics and demographics. Pastors are asked frequently, "How many members do you have at your church?" Repeatedly, congregations are compared and their success is measured by size. It is terribly unfair and unrealistic to expect a church in a rural area to grow to magnificent proportions.

It's foolish to ignore the role of demographics in predicting how large a church will grow. No matter how dedicated a church is, if the ministry area only has a thousand people it, the church will never be large. It's not the pastor's fault, nor is it a lack of commitment on part of the congregation. It's simple arithmetic.

Many books and seminars over-emphasize churches that are located in large demographic areas. A pastor who is revitalizing a church is probably not in a mega church. Frankly, there is no comparison. Our competition is not with other churches, but with Satan.

To be realistic, you need to focus on the percentage of population being reached, not the actual numbers. It is unwise and unhelpful to compare attendance between churches. Every church has a unique fishing pond, and each pond is stocked with a different number and type of fish. It's like comparing tangerines and submarines: Two churches may sound a lot alike, but in taking a closer look, their differences will be obvious. What is your church's specific mission?

33. Count the cost of growth. The revitalizer should be realistic about the cost of growth. Usually when there is a major change in the church some people will leave. The make-up of one of my churches in 2004 was very different from when I first arrived in 1990. I found a photo I had taken of the congregation during a Sunday morning worship service and was amazed at how many people are no longer attending! To see the change in members is sad, but it was bound to happen. Part of the change is due to life transitions. Some have since died, others have moved out of the area, many of the children have married or gone to college, and others have left because they could not accept the changes to the church.

There is also a financial cost to growth. It takes money to grow a church because ministry is not cheap. Any churchman can tell you about how the annual budget increases each year just to maintain the church facilities. The increases do not include advertising, Vacation Bible School, youth activities, big events, and additional money necessary for creating new ministries.

34. Expect quality. Always look for ways to improve the quality of the Sunday morning service. A well organized worship service, good sound equipment, nice hymn books, a digital projector, a nice bulletin, an enthusiastic announcer, quality musicianship, upbeat music, new carpet, new sanctuary chairs, a stage large enough for musical theater and skits.

There is a lack of quality in many small churches. The church should attempt to do the best it can. Always evaluate if there is room for improvement. Ask newcomers for suggestions. When we have been at the church for a long time we tend to overlook things that need painted or repaired. Does the piano need tuning? Is it time to change the bulletin layout? How is the sound? Can everyone hear? Don't let just anyone sing a music "special", especially people who cannot sing.

Small churches are notorious for having spontaneous solos from someone who "felt led" to do a song. I have been embarrassed by a music special. When I hear the singer say, "Bear with me, I haven't had time to practice," I read the bulletin. If you happen to have that dear saint who likes to sing every other week, diplomatically ask them if they mind letting others have an opportunity. In my first church, we had a needy person who always wanted to sing a song "she wrote." It was amazing how all her songs sounded like Dottie Rambo's! We worked around this problem by having her sing in the choir – only.

35. Break out of the single cell. It is no secret that small churches are a "single cell" organism. A single cell church is a congregation that has not yet passed the turning point and become a true organization; the term "cell" corresponds roughly to the natural social unit of 150 or fewer. People want to know everyone's name because they pride themselves on being "one big happy family".

I found this one of my major challenges. A small church has gotten comfortable with being a small group. Everybody knows everybody! One way I approached this phenomenon was to expand entryways into the church fellowship. When more people started coming I involved them as soon as they were assimilated. New members help change the pattern that has developed by introducing their ideas. Those ideas led to adding ministries that interested other people outside the church.

A retired pastor who joined the church asked me if it was okay for him to start having a "senior luncheon" for retirees at the church. I was so relieved! I made sure he had at his disposal whatever he needed. It wasn't long before the luncheon averaged two dozen people.

Another way to break out of the single cell is to start a second worship service. Gary McIntosh writes,

> Perhaps the number one way that a small church breaks out of its single cell orientation into a multiple cell orientation is by adding a second worship service. In addition, multiple worship services aid the growth of a small church by providing options, expanding space, increasing the church's faith, enlarging ministry, and reaching new people.

Bill Easum also talks about breaking out of the single cell in a number of his books. In his article, *"Breaking the 300 Barrier"*, Easum talks extensively about getting past the single cell mentality.

> You must move beyond the "Single Cell" mentality. The single cell issue is "we are one big happy family." This is why people respond to the idea of a second worship service by saying, "But we won't know everyone anymore." This is seldom overcome until a church reaches 500 in worship. The small church acts as a family. The large church acts as a family of families.

There will be limitations to growth if the church does not intentionally create and develop a small group or cell ministry.

WHAT IS THE BEST STRATEGY?

I believe that the revitalization movement has been good for the church for a number of reasons. *First*, it has challenged the local church to have an outward focus, especially in the area of evangelism. *Second*, the success of newly planted churches has shown existing congregations what is possible if they are open to paradigms shifts. Society is changing rapidly, but the church is often slow to adjust and thereby becomes irrelevant.

I do not think there is a "best" strategy. I do not believe God will honor any notions conceived by man that do not ultimately glorify Him. I have listed what has worked for me in the two declining churches I have led and in the other congregations where I have attended. I think these suggestions are just common sense to most transformational leaders and they will have an impact if the pastor methodically applies them.

However, no methodological approach to church renewal will work if the Holy Spirit is not in it. The church must be willing to change again and again. The pastor must not become comfortable with past successes. He must continually prepare himself and his congregational leaders to embrace and support new innovative ventures when the opportunities arise. The change process never truly stops. The amount of energy that must be poured into the process may be less and the urgency level may decline after its initial peak, but a congregation that decides to rest on its laurels is taking the first step toward decline.

CHAPTER 4   CAUTION SIGNS

When driving, we come upon caution signs on the highway notifying us to watch for hazards ahead. There are times when I don't pay attention to warnings as I should. At the beginning of my ministry, I wish I had been aware of certain warning signs in the church.

Most members are related. A family church usually is a clan operation. Because new people cannot become a part of the family, growth will always be hindered by the mere existence of the clan's ownership. "Koinonitis" is a fatal disease. Also, when two families are competing in the church for power, there is no way the church can be healthy. This is a common ailment in rural congregations. Unless there is an influx of people to offset the influence of the biologically related, the pastor will always have to work in the permission-giving structure of the family's choosing. If possible, discuss your concern with the key family members regarding a closed club.

My first church was located in a large city but was dominated by people from one family who lived outside the city. Most of the family made up the core group. Every Sunday they all went to a restaurant together after the Sunday worship service. I don't think they were aware of the impact of not including others. My family and I were rarely asked to join them and they never asked the new attendees, either. This was "koinonitis" run amok.

According to Peter Wagner,

> Koinonitis is when Christians develop "koinonia" or fellowship to such an exaggerated extent that all their attention and energies are being absorbed by other Christians, evangelistic myopia is likely to settle in. The lost are out there around the church, but they no longer are a high priority. Even when new people come into the church, the fellowship circles have been so rigidly defined that the new people cannot fit it. Strangers are a threat to churches with koinonitis.

I was at this church for four years. It only had seventeen people when I arrived. When I left, there were eighty in regular attendance. I will always remember our last congregational meeting with them. One of the older family members mentioned that we had enough people coming to the church, and there was no need to build a new sanctuary, even though there were times the room was full. I will never forget watching her as she said, "We have enough people, you know? If we just keep the people we've got and try to get to know each other better, things will go well. I don't see the need to go into debt. Really, we have enough now. I think we'll be fine." I watched them all nod with approval. I realized that this matter had already been discussed among them and that she was trying to convince me to agree. However, that night I knew that I had taken the small congregation as far as they were willing to go. I am no chaplain. We made plans for an organized exit.

National Politics. People are usually passionate about their political views. We have heard that we should avoid discussing politics and religion at family gatherings. That is good advice. There is nothing wrong with being involved in the political process, and people should vote regularly. But emphasizing one political party over another in the fellowship may create unnecessary conflict. I have had individuals who passed out political literature and alienated new people and fostered heated debate. Discourage campaign buttons, flyers, or any material that may stir up strife. On the other hand, people in the congregation tend to agree on certain moral convictions, particularly if the pastor has discussed his ideas. There is no need for the pastor to shy away from sharing his opinions as long as he knows to be diplomatic and "agree to disagree." Politicians come and go, but Jesus Christ is our King.

Majoring on secondary issues. Preaching the Gospel and making disciples should be the main purpose of the church. Some churches become distracted by subjects that are important but detract from the mission of the church and cause divisions in the fellowship. Secondary issues such as which version of the Bible to use, dancing, drinking alcohol, music, end-times theology, whether women should wear pants, speaking in tongues, politics, sports, home school or public school may take your attention away from your mission.

We recognize the differences between various members of the church family, and many of these differences give us a good laugh and nothing more. Yet we must also recognize that there are genuine divisions among us, some of them hostile and harmful. What's worse, there are not only divisions among different Christian groups - many times the sharpest divisions can be found right within the same church.

It is a blessing to see two brothers or sisters sharply differ on a particular subject, but express that their friendship is more important than their preferences or opinion.

As a pastor once said, "Life gets frustrating when we fail to discern the non-essentials from the essentials of our faith. God's church is often of not much help because she tends to bicker over trivial matters of conscience instead of building God's people in the fundamental teachings of Christ."

Criticizing the former pastor. Pastors should always find something nice to say about their predecessors. By belittling one's predecessor, the pastor is setting himself up for criticism. You do not know what circumstances or personalities the former pastor encountered. It is too easy to criticize others to make ourselves look better. If we sow criticism of the former pastor, we open ourselves up to criticism. Speak well of them.

Depending on the congregation's experience with their previous ministers, I think it is healthy for a former pastor to visit. At my first church, I invited a minister who had served years before me. He told me later how much it meant to be welcomed back.

If successful, don't crow – if defeated, don't croak. Many situations can cause a pastor to croak. Usually it's not the routine of ministry that is difficult, it's dealing with antagonists. Satan comes to steal, kill, and destroy – and he comes after the shepherd first. Most pastors I know who have left the ministry resigned due to criticism or political maneuverings by church members. Jesus knows what it is like. After all, he was betrayed by a member of his own small band.

There are seasons when everything goes well. Goals are reached, planned endeavors are crowned with success, the Spirit moves. Souls are saved and saints blessed. In these times, the mature leader knows on whose brow to place the crown of achievement.

The toughest and most rewarding job in the world is that of the pastor. The pastor has the greatest influence in the local community. The pastor has to be all things to all people without compromising his calling. There will be times when the pastor feels like quitting

Every pastor experiences times of discouragement. The pastor must try to create a support group. Not "yes" people, but loyal supporters. Find non-critical listeners. Experienced pastors are especially helpful because they know what you are going through. They know the reality of ministry. They know what questions to ask.

Many church histories have a long-suffering pastor who had patiently faced a difficult situation. About him, James Rutz comments,

> Sometimes the #1 victim of the system, the loneliest one of all, is the guy who is trying the hardest to make it all work. Don't blame him! He beats his brains out in the pulpit week after week to make a difference in people's lives. But sometimes he feels like he's been condemned to a lifetime of futility, trying in vain to motivate a sullen pack of foot-dragging spiritual adolescents who never quite seem to see the big picture, never get excited enough to shoulder responsibilities, and never (by the way) come anywhere close to a 10% tithe.

The African-American Methodist pastor, Zan Wesley Holmes, reminds us: "Those whom God ordains, God sustains."

CHAPTER 5   AN EXAMPLE OF WHAT NOT TO DO

"A man convinced against his will, is of the same opinion still." ~ Benjamin Franklin

I met the young pastor not long after he arrived at the nearby church. About thirty people had worshiped there for many of years. The founding pastor had retired but the former pastor's siblings stayed and made up the core of the church. The family was in charge of the music and did most of the work.

It was not long before the new pastor began telling me what was wrong with the church. According to him, the people did not know how to worship. When I asked him what kind of music they liked he said, "That old Country-Gospel junk." I realized that he was not willing to work within the congregation's culture. The church was made up of people who were middle-aged, not highly educated, who held strongly onto older Pentecostal distinctives.

I wanted to give him some encouragement and advice but I primarily listened because he was so upset. I felt that he would force changes onto the congregation whether they liked them or not. Even though they liked to sing old-time hymns, he insisted that they sing contemporary praise & worship music. When he tried to blend the music styles, he was disturbed that they liked the old hymns better. I suggested that he do more of their kind of music. He said he would think about it.

Eventually, people started to leave. First, it was the former pastor's family who transferred to another church. He was so glad that he did not have to listen to the "sisters" lead and sing their music anymore. The next group to leave was the elderly who missed the sisters and the hymns they used to sing.

The young pastor drove a new red Pontiac Firebird, and he and his wife dressed and acted much younger than they were. I thought they were just out of Bible college and were in their twenties. One day I learned that they were in their mid-thirties! His immaturity had lost him respect among the adults. My wife and I were trying to hint to them that they needed to adjust their lifestyle. He was not willing to work part-time when the congregation was clearly unable to support him.

There was $12,000 in the church's savings account. But he was spending the church's money on things they could not afford - like new sound equipment, weightlifting apparatus, an old van, and other gadgetry. It occurred to me that he was trying to attract new people, but he was going about it the wrong way. He was not mobilizing the people he had. He led the singing, preached the sermon, gave the announcements, and took up the offering.

He did not realize that he was a cross-cultural missionary. He did not seem to understand contextualization. He was trying to attract a crowd that did not share the same style as the people who worshiped there. As a result, there were no new people replacing the old members who were leaving. The congregation had an image problem with no chance of recovery.

One Monday, he came to my house to announce that they were closing the church and that he was looking for another church. He said that they only had five people the Sunday before and that it was obviously over. I prayed for him and wished him well. He thanked me for listening and encouraging him. There was little I could say. I had known this day was coming. I was saddened that things did not work out. The denomination sold the building.

CHAPTER 6   THE WINNING COACH ANALOGY

How athletic coaching principles can be applied to pastoral leadership.

The sport of football is a great example of a coordinated group effort. It takes hours of practicing fundamental techniques, communication, and coordinated plans for advancing the football. Each player on the team specializes in a specific skill. The offense in particular illustrates how everyone on the field must work together in order to score a touchdown. The linemen must know their blocking assignments on each play so that no pass rusher can get to the quarterback. If the team is planning a running play, the tailback will need to go through the gap that the linemen created. Each organized play is a detailed predetermined plan with specific coordinated movements for each player.

Coaches in the National Football League are frequently hired to take on a faltering program and turn it around in a few seasons. Surely, there are pastor-coaches who can do the same thing on a church level. Just as it has been recognized that there is an apostolic gift, there must be a revitalizer gift. But what exactly is the role of leadership in the revitalization of existing churches? Can it be assumed that as a person is evaluated and later trained for church planting, that there are pastors/coaches who are gifted at turning around a "losing" church?

A coach may spend hours preparing his team for the game, but he does not play the game. He is not on the field the day of the game. He is not blocking, tackling, passing, or running with the football. He has equipped his team to win. In his book, *Beyond Church Growth*, Robert Logan makes the same analogy when he wrote, "As a sports fan, I realize how much similarity exists between the job of a pastor and that of a coach. Just as a coach equips his or her team to win, so an effective pastor functions like a coach to cultivate a thriving congregation."

Like any good coach, the pastor has a game plan. According to Logan, effective coaches share six common characteristics:

They establish challenging but attainable goals.

They recruit athletes for the team.
They inspire the team to maximum performance.
They design a strategy.
They conduct team practices.
They cultivate team spirit in a winning environment.

People like to be on a winning team. Whether we like it or not, people are attracted to a winning team. Just look at the fan base of winning teams. Sports teams with a history of winning championships display their banners publicly to remind the team and their fans that they have a winning tradition. The banners also communicate to the visitor that the team has won in the past and will probably win again. A team with a history of losing usually does not have any banners or signs posted that point to success. This is the challenge facing the pastor - teaching the church how to win, that the church can do far more than it thinks it can. That it will be used by God to make an impact for Christ.

When I was in high school, the football team had a record of five wins and five loses, and a long history of mediocre seasons. The team had grown accustomed to losing. When a new coach was hired, he set out to change the attitude of his players. The first thing he did was recruit every young man on campus to play football, whether or not he had played before. He was looking for naturally talented athletes to play a sport that they had not played before.

He made it a goal to know each boy by name and speak to him when he met him in the hall. On the first day of summer practice, he told the entire team that their goal was not to have a winning season, but to win the district championship, and in order for that to happen there were going to be some changes.

The coach introduced new plays and made it clear the fundamentals that made the difference. All the boys were expected to get in shape, practice hard, and come together as a team. He introduced cheering and clapping for teammates in practice. He made physical changes: the locker room was repainted and new carpet was installed, and he did something that seemed impossible, he had the school buy new uniforms. Each player wore the same style socks, practice shoes and game shoes. He was once heard saying, "A team has to look like a team, act like a team, and play like a team. And boys, football is a team sport. No individual ever wins a game by himself. Y'all can only win if you play as a team."

Within two years, the team won the district title and was in the state playoffs year after year. The players didn't have more talent than the others before them. What was the difference? To this day, the school has a winning tradition because he laid down the foundation for success.

When a revitalizer arrives, he dwells on the positive and on what God is going to do. He talks about his vision, recruits and trains his team, upgrades the facilities, preaches the fundamentals of the faith, encourages practice, and expects his team to win on the ministry field. If he does his job well the congregation will have new life and a winning tradition because he laid down the foundation for success.

I have taken the winning coach analogy and broken it down to five specific areas:

The Coach Pastor as a pacesetter. Printed on a T-shirt in a shop in Quantico, Virginia, "Never underestimate the power of a group of people who believe nothing can keep them from success and who are willing to do anything to achieve it." What would happen if this were the attitude of the local church?

The pastor needs to be a self-starter. If he expects his team to play hard then he should set the pace by being a hard worker. He cannot be lazy. A good coach spends hours planning his strategy and his game plan. He studies game films, meets with his staff, and tries to determine how to use each player.

His preparation is vital to the team's success because he knows his team's strengths and weaknesses and he will try to adjust to the next game situation. Because he is proud of his team, he knows each player's position, jersey number, ability, height, weight, and how to play him.

As the pacesetter, the pastor-coach is a competitor. He does not accept defeat because he always plans to win and his players sense it.

When the players are on the practice field, they know he expects them to know their blocking assignments. The coach runs the plays repeatedly until they perform them correctly. A winning coach never lets up on his team by allowing his players to accept mediocrity. He wants his team to be polished like a well-oiled machine. When it is time for the game the team will be prepared and will feel confident when they walk on the field.

The Coach Pastor as an encourager. The reason many people do not get involved in church is because they think they have nothing to offer. Some do not believe that they are good enough to try-out for the team. They are afraid to try because they are afraid of failing or making mistakes. The pastor must be someone who believes in people and will cheer them on even they puts forth the smallest effort. A new pastor may find that people in his church have not been encouraged to get involved.

It is so important that everyone knows that their efforts are appreciated and not taken for granted. Dexter Yager makes this point when he writes, "Make a point to find something good. Then observe it out loud. Praise is something people are deeply hungry for but seldom get to taste. If you are willing to give it, people will begin to gravitate toward you."

It may seem elementary, but the pastor's words of public praise go a long way to encouraging others to participate. During the Sunday morning service, I presented the "official" church pen to individuals for their involvement in church and in ministries outside the congregation. The pastor mentions specifically the work that has been done and thanks them for their service. The congregation claps and cheers in appreciation. Doing such a simple act of acknowledgment goes a long way to build volunteers. There have been times when the person weeps because it was the first time in their life that they have ever received praise for their efforts in anything.

It is important to teach people about *"failing forward"*, a term coined by John C. Maxwell, regarding the need to learn from one's mistakes and to build upon them. Maxwell encourages the reader to embrace the value of failure as a teacher. As long as we learn from

60

our mistakes and do not give up, we are making progress toward our goals, or failing forward. When we do convince an individual to attempt something new, we should be prepared to build them up if things do not meet their own personal expectations.

A winning coach will not only tell his players what they need to work on, he will also find ways to build the confidence in his team by encouraging them - especially after a loss. A winning pastor will train his church, his team, to win by trying.

The Coach Pastor as an equipper. For too long the church has depended upon the "professional" pastor who acted as an enabler rather than an equipper. According to Richard Hutcheson, "An enabler or facilitator is a relatively uninvolved technician who understands the process by which things are accomplished and enables others to achieve goals." In short, the enabler almost becomes a bystander, asking, "What do you all want me to do?" Lyle Schaller said, "We found the word enabler was a synonym for not being an initiator, not calling, not being aggressive, not taking leadership responsibilities." The opposite of an enabler is equipper. Peter Wagner defines an equipper as

> A leader who actively sets goals for a congregation according to the will of God, obtains goal ownership from the people, and sees that each church member is properly motivated and equipped to do his or her part in accomplishing the goals.

When the pastor encourages the people to discover their spiritual gifts and operate in them, he opens up all kinds of possibilities.

The Coach Pastor as a visionary. I remember seeking God for a vision before I was to begin as the pastor of one of my churches. One day, I had a flood of ideas comes rushing in my mind. I had to hurry and write down the ten-point plan God gave me before I forgot it. I had a sense of joy as I quietly wept thanking God for answering my prayer. It was wonderful to have a vision and a plan for the church.

Vision is the God given plan for the leader and the ministry that God has laid on the heart and mind for that individual and group. It is the clear path on which a particular church functions and operates. It focuses all of the congregation's activity under a joint purpose, directed by one question, "What has God directed us to do and what actions should we take to fulfill God's plan for us?"

It takes patience to lay a foundation for change, especially when dealing with influential individuals who may limit the pastor's activity. The church is not quite a business corporation where the pastor can give orders like a CEO. Perhaps with the exception of a younger church, the longer an established congregation exists the more difficult it is for a new pastor to introduce change.

Some denominational executives assume that pastors are automatically leaders and therefore do not need to talk about how vision is absent if there is no leader to bring vision. In order for vision to come into fruition, a church leader must have leadership competence. As John Maxwell often states in his seminar, "Look over your shoulder. If nobody is following you, you are not a leader." Vision and leadership are linked together and need to be connected in the same sentence.

The Holy Spirit is the catalyst for the pastor's dream and vision for his church and his ministry. God has called pastors to a particular work and a course of action in the setting God has placed them. God wants church leaders to be Holy Spirit led and Holy Spirit driven.

The Coach Pastor as an innovator. The winning coach is always looking for new innovative ideas. When he sees one that can be applied to his situation, he tries to find ways to integrate it into his church. People get excited when they are permitted to do church in a new way. It is the coach's job to let go of preconceived thoughts of how church ought to be done. Some of the most creative ideas come from the regular person who is in tune with the leading of the Holy Spirit. A good coach is waiting to hear God speak through some of the most unlikely individuals who suddenly "had a thought" about how something can be done.

The winning coach knows that it takes teamwork and that he must be flexible to follow the leading of the Holy Spirit. By listening for what God wants to do among his people, church ministry never becomes outmoded or tries to put God in a box.

CHAPTER 7   ANTAGONISTS AND MS. OWN-A-PEW

"Drive out the mocker, and out goes strife; quarrels and insults are ended." Proverbs 22:10

Pride, pride,
Eating away like a cancer inside,
Taking the place where love did abide,
Pride, pride.

The purpose of this chapter is to discuss the antagonists that a church revitalizer, or any pastor, will probably encounter. Before growth can occur in the declining church, all barriers must be confronted, including people who stand in the way of change. In an established church, it may be a long-term member who has gained control by combative means. In other situations, it may an aggressive person who is somewhat new to the fellowship and is initiating trouble. Either way, those who lead the church must use their authority effectively to address the situation.

I think one of the best books written about antagonists is Kenneth Haugk's, *Antagonists in the Church*. Haugk showed me how to identify antagonists and deal with them. His book should be required reading at all seminaries and ought to be read by every pastor and church leader. I like Haugk's insightful commentary because his practical wisdom has been so helpful to me. Haugk's definition of an antagonist:

> Antagonists are individuals who, based on non-substantive evidence, go out of their way to make insatiable demands, usually attacking the person or performance of others. These attacks are selfish in nature, tearing down rather than building up, and are frequently directed against those in a leadership capacity.

Seminary professors generally do not discuss dealing with antagonists in the church. As a result, many pastors are ill prepared to face the obstacle of a bully. Yet, in the two congregations I have pastored, I have had to confront antagonists. Not only did they cause me great stress, they influenced or harassed people into doubting my leadership and vision. There is a God-given authority to the pastoral calling. If the pastor has a vision and calling from God, he will stay true to that call. My calling gave me the determination to stand up against selfish troublemakers.

Proverbs 22:10 is my mandate from God to confront or even expel the troublemaker who wounds the sheep or is constantly at the center of most conflicts. Any person who destroys reputations, practices hostile gossip, attempts to create factions, and carries a continually ungodly attitude toward church leadership should be removed as quickly as possible.

I personally knew of one man who was so difficult that he contributed to a fine pastor's decision to leave the ministry. Over the years, several other pastors in various area churches were also caused great emotional harm due to his critical spirit. He moved from church to church attacking each pastor. He was well read and a loud debater. He would stay for a few years until the pastor or the church leadership told him to leave. How much more problematic is it for the pastor when there is a long-term bully in the congregation? If the pastor will not stand up to such a person, he is in for a long stressful time.

When it comes to church revitalization, the wise pastor will anticipate someone will need to leave the fellowship. Bill Easum is another church growth consultant who has written extensively about the individuals or bullies who oppose the pastor at every turn and hinder growth in the church. Easum is blunt and unapologetic about facing problematic bullies.

> I am convinced that most church people think that one of the tenets of Christianity is being nice. Too many church people think pastors should be nice people and churches are supposed to be nice places where people live harmoniously together. As a result, most church leaders never really say what they feel or think, which leads to loss of community and a handful of dysfunctional controllers who keep the majority of people intimidated. Niceness leads to the withholding of information, manipulation of people and events, and gossip. I've discovered that the most dangerous gatekeepers often appear to be nice.

64

Why is not being nice so important that it is included in the list of leadership clues for the wormhole? Because most dying churches have a handful of people who need to be kicked in the butt. That's why.

I will never forget the older wealthy woman who stuck her finger in my face and said, "If I leave this church it will fold." I had only been the pastor of my first church for a month when I received her threat in front of a group of people after the Sunday morning service. Everyone around me got nervous and quiet. I did not understand why she was angry. In my sermon, I mentioned to the congregation that God wanted to do some great ministry among them and that they would see their numbers grow if they honored God and prayed. I guess the woman did not like the fact that God did not ask her permission.

My first reaction was to be nice to her and try to calm her down. I was not about to pour gas on the female flamethrower! I remember trying to determine what the center of her opposition was. The best thing I could do was not let her throw me into a panic or allow myself to show any kind of fear. God had given me on-the-job training a few years earlier when I was a personnel manager in a poultry plant. Every day I had dealt with demanding people - from union representatives to disgruntled employees. Fortunately for me, I had seen this pushy attitude before and I was not startled by her demagoguery. My main concern was that I carry myself in a mature fashion because I knew I had to look unmoved while the others were looking on.

That night I received several phone calls from people who were apologizing for the way she attacked me. They thought I handled myself well and said, "Everyone at the church usually runs from her", and that I should do the same. The truth is I am not one to run from conflict, but I had more to lose than she did so I held my tongue. If, however, she had regularly attacked me in front of the church over a period of a few Sundays, I know I would have confronted her. As far as I was concerned, she could keep her checkbook at home, and I said so to the people who had called me. Bill Easum further states:

Being nice is not what Jesus wants from any of us. One of the basic lessons I'm learning as a consultant is that before renewal begins in a church or denomination, it is normal that someone has to leave or be denied. Almost every time a dying church attempts to thrive once again, someone tries to bully the leadership out of the attempt. And almost every time, if a turn around is to take place, such persons are lost along the way because they are no longer allowed to get their way. When they can't get their way, they leave. Not even Jesus got through the journey with all of their disciples. Why should we expect to?

The woman did not come to church often because she traveled to Florida frequently. Not long after she challenged me she was away for a few weeks. Then one Sunday, after she had returned from another Florida trip, we were sitting around at a church potluck when she yelled across the room, "I ran into Mrs. Smith in Florida. Do you know her? Well, she said that you used to attend a Bible study in her home and that you were a fine young man, and that we are blessed to have you here." It was obvious that God had intervened in my behalf.

Of course, not everyone who disagrees with the pastor is an antagonist. The pastor will not always be right nor will he do and say the right thing one hundred percent of the time. He should be approached and receive correction if he is out of order. On other occasions, there will be church members who make suggestions regarding changes to programs and may question the pastor's decisions in some situations. One grousing member is not a reason to preach a fiery sermon or a cause to resign. The majority are usually fair-minded in their expectations. Trust the evaluation of the many over the judgment of a few. This does not imply that these well meaning people are "going against" the pastor or trying to show disrespect. Experienced pastors have learned the difference between involved teammates and troublemakers. As Haugk cautions, "Antagonism should not be confused with mere criticism or healthy conflict in the church." Healthy churches are honorable in their disagreements and highly prize the love of God in the fellowship.

It is assured that a pastor will eventually face opposition of some kind in his ministry. Even the most gifted pastor will encounter situations that cause him to doubt himself and perhaps even leave his church. However, if the pastor has a plan of action for moving the church forward, he will remember to step back and assess why he is being challenged. Dexter Yager, *Dynamic People Skills*, reminds us of what Abraham Lincoln went through,

> Don't ever believe in the opposition more than you believe in yourself. When people criticize you, it's vital not to sell out to their point of view. Every great leader has to plow through opposition and ridicule in order to achieve a dream. When Abraham Lincoln became active in politics and ran for the presidency, newspapers around the country called him "the old baboon" and "that ape, Abraham Lincoln."

If there are gatekeepers who are not cooperative, try to reason with them or try to work around them. If the gatekeepers are powerful, insist on being in control, and reject the pastor's attempts at revitalization, the pastor should plan to leave and go to a receptive church. There is nothing gained by putting oneself through such misery. On the other hand, if the pastor is confident that God has called him to a particular church, then he had better prayerfully prepare himself. Few church consultants have spoken more plainly about antagonists than Bill Easum.

> Throughout all of my consulting ministry, I have seen a disturbing pattern ... most established churches are held hostage by one or two bullies. Some individual or small group of individuals are usually extremely opposed to the church making any radical change, even if it means the change would give the church a chance to thrive once again. I keep hearing pastors say, "If I tried that, I'd lose my job!" Courageous pastors often ask, "What do I do when one person intimidates the church so much that it is not willing to try something new?" My response is always, "Either convert them, neutralize them, kick them out, or kill them. The Body can not live with cancer." To which someone usually cries, "That's not very Christian!"

If a bully causes church members to cower, the pastor should develop a strategy for removing the individual. First, I would sit down with my Overseer or Bishop and explain every detail on the assumption that the antagonist will probably contact the Overseer. It is important that the pastor tell the facts as accurately as possible and not embellish his story. He should also humbly seek the Overseer's advice. By doing so, the pastor gains credibility with the Overseer and prevents the antagonist from negatively affecting his opinion of the pastor.

I think the worst thing a pastor can do is show weakness. The pastor should be slow to anger and slow to go to battle with an antagonist. On the other hand, it has helped me when an antagonist learned that I have a "protector" personality, because they think twice about initiating conflict. Perhaps it is not good to have that sort of reputation, but it has come in handy when confronting troublemakers. I believe it is better to confront the problem than to let it fester.

Because there has been an emphasis on "servant leadership" in the church, too many pastors are appeasers who are not willing to confront wolves in the church. I have been dismayed at how my fellow pastors allowed themselves to be pushed around by forceful parishioners. Easum has observed the same timidity.

> I'm convinced that one of the main sins of the established church is that we have taught ourselves to be nice instead of being Christian. In spite of aspiring to be a disciple of Jesus, we teach that the essence of Christianity is to be nice. Where do we get such a notion? Certainly not from the actions of Jesus.

> In the absence of crisis, many people would give high marks to likeability. But when a crisis occurs, people want leadership, not affability. People may not like strong leaders, but they hate weak ones. Certainly, a potential antagonist will dislike effective actions you take to oppose him or her, and will therefore dislike you. Further, others in the congregation might like-wise express discomfort with your firm actions.

In the late 1990s, I went through was one of the most trying periods of my pastoral ministry. During this time, we had several problems arise. A woman left her husband because of his emotional and controlling abuse. He threatened my life because he blamed me for her leaving.

In the midst of the above-mentioned situation, I had two major wolves in the church who were judgmental gossips and busybodies. In the case with the abused wife, one of the antagonists told me that I was not handling the problem correctly. She and her husband began taking the abuser's side and criticizing the woman to others. The antagonist had convinced her husband to meet with me to explain that divorce was wrong no matter the circumstances (they did not care that the man was mentally unstable and dangerous). I had dealt with this antagonist before. She often gave long speeches about what was wrong with our church and gave negative evaluations of our leadership. She usually approached me with a concerned, syrupy voice, "Pastor, can I ask you a question? I have a concern." She would then take a verbal stab at me, followed by, "We love you, Pastor." The woman and her husband finally left after several people told them they were out of line.

The other antagonist disliked me because I stood firm. She spent hours on the phone. She was raised in a church and knew all the Christian clichés to use in her "prayer requests". She gossiped to such a degree that at one point I had a list of fifteen people who accused her of gossiping about them and wanted her removed. My elders and I met with her and her husband alone in hope that she would quell her gossip. I saw her grab a teenager one morning and shake her because she did not like what she was wearing. She once called one of our elders to disparage me. The elder told her to talk to me if she had a complaint. She said, "He won't run." The elder said, "Pardon me?" He laughed at how she gave herself away with a slip of the tongue.

Antagonists do not like pastors who are strong leaders. When I think I have spotted an antagonist, I watch them constantly. I listen for any gossip or continuing criticism about my team or me. Haugk says, "Leaders must take a firm (even unpopular) stand in order to effectively prevent antagonistic situations." I believe it is a mistake for a pastor not to respond quickly to manipulation from new people.

One Easter Sunday, immediately after I had delivered my message and closed the service, a visitor approached me and said, "I am disappointed in your message. I was expecting something else." I listened intensely and simply replied, "I am sorry, madam, but I don't know who you are. But, I try to preach what God has placed on my heart."

On another occasion a visitor came to my Sunday School class said, "I am here to straighten out the pastor." At first, it didn't register to me what he said. I don't think he knew that I was the pastor. So, I asked him to repeat what he said. Then I told him that he is not the Holy Spirit and that I have elders, a Church Council, and an Overseer to discipline me if I need it. We were all relieved that he did not return. We had never heard such bold aggression before.

In my encounters with antagonists, I have observed these common characteristics:

> A condescending attitude toward the pastor or the church. They are disrespectful of the congregation's ministry. They may belittle the worship, criticize the operation of the Sunday School, or give unsolicited advice in a manner that impugns the work of others.

> They are "spooky spiritual". They see themselves as having special theological knowledge pertaining to the faith. They expect to see a demon in everything. They use the phrase, "The Lord told me to tell you..." when talking to the pastor. They believe that if someone doesn't receive a healing from God that the person lacks faith or is in sin. Some people believe that the King James Version is the only acceptable translation. They are arrogant and self-serving. They want to be seen in public as having great Bible knowledge. Rarely do they volunteer for dirty work.

> They are "expert" teachers. They love to challenge the Sunday School teacher. It is not uncommon for them to question the pastor's sermon and find fault with it.

> They are more likely to be married to a weak spouse whom they control. In my experiences, it was a weak husband. The

weak husband is usually quiet and "hen-pecked".

They are dysfunctional emotionally or mentally. Some are church hoppers who move from church to church looking for the next movement of God.

They are secretive. They practice guerrilla warfare. Often they will stop talking when the pastor enters the room. If the pastor is feeling paranoid, perhaps the feeling is justified. They often whisper.

They will not submit to the authority of the pastor. They may give lip service to the pastor's position but question his teaching. They insinuate that there is a leadership vacuum and that there are no "spiritual leaders" in the church. They will mock the pastor's authority when they think it is safe to do so in front of others.

My strategy when dealing with an antagonist:

Leave no "paper trail". Never write anything that can be used against you. Especially no emails.

Go to your most trusted and loyal advisors in the church immediately and seek their advice. Determine if the antagonist has a legitimate compliant.

Do not exhibit anger and guard your tongue. Do not criticize them in public. Do not say anything about them or hint from the pulpit that there is a problem.

Find out whom they are talking to in order to do "damage control". Circle the core group wagons. Trust that you are not the only person who sees the problem.

When a church member passes along the gossip and slander from the antagonist to you do not excuse or justify their behavior in your response but rather say things like, "It saddens me to hear that so & so said that. I love them and I am their friend."

Be patient and allow the truth to reveal itself. Be careful about how you defend yourself. Trust God.

71

Have a witness with you if you meet with them privately.

Watch them closely. They have revealed their lack of character.

Contact denominational leadership if necessary. But if you do, do not exhibit an ungodly attitude lest you give the appearance that you are a perpetrator.

Antagonists tend to speak as if they are representing a group of people. They believe it gives them credibility and power. I have learned to ask for specifics when they say, "Everybody says". I ask them to clarify who "everybody" is because to say they are speaking for everybody is an exaggeration. I used to panic when someone would tell me that "everyone" thinks I should do such and such, until I considered who may disagree with their view. H. B. London gives some wise advice on this matter.

Try not to over generalize about either the critic or the affirmer. The work of the church is shot through with the notion that one vocal person speaks for the several or many. More often than not, they speak for themselves only and almost never for God. It is good to remind yourself that even difficult people have no pastor but you, so they need your acceptance and forbearance.

I think most antagonists have less power to manipulate and create dissension in a larger church. In a smaller church, they are a big fish in a small pond. In a small church, a pastor is more accessible and open to direct confrontation. Of course, this does not mean that antagonists are relegated to small churches alone, but they receive more attention and have a larger impact in a smaller setting. London continues, "Because congregations are often relatively small, they are ideal places for antagonists to gain the attention they crave. Congregations in the United States consist of an average of 125 members. It is an axiom that the smaller an organization is, the more vulnerable it is to attack."

Haugk mentions three kinds of antagonists: *Moderate* antagonists lack the self-starting quality and perseverance of the other types. They have personality problems. *Major* antagonists are not as severely disturbed as hardcore antagonists, yet they exhibit similar behaviors.

Major antagonists *refuse* to be reasoned with and are insatiable. *Hardcore* antagonists *cannot* be reasoned with because they lack the emotional stability to understand. They are seriously disturbed individuals. They tend to have incredible tenacity and an unbelievable desire to make trouble.

In chapters nine and ten, Haugk has written a practical guide on how to recognize antagonists. He opens the chapter by saying, "Just as antagonists reveal themselves by their red flags, they also exhibit warning signs that telegraph their intentions to begin an attack...By alerting yourself to the earliest stages of an attack, you gain an advantage." The following warning signs are helpful after an antagonist has been identified by the pastor.

EARLY WARNING SIGNS:

A chill in the relationship - a person exhibits red flags by changes in his or her manner of relating to you. In group situations, the antagonist might show disrespect toward you, use biting sarcasm.

Honeyed "concerns" - they might pay you a visit or send a letter of "concern." This is an attempt to control the pastor.

Nettlesome questions - they begin by asking picky questions. You find yourself feeling nettled as the antagonist becomes a constant fly-in-the-ointment.

Mobilizing forces and pot-stirring - they gather support and create discord, conflict, and doubt.

Meddling in areas that are not their concern. They may think they have the right to keep people "in line" or give unsolicited advice.

Resistance - defying the pastor's authority, blocking the approval of certain matters that ordinarily glide through the governing machinery with ease.

LATER WARNING SIGNS:

Sloganeering - use one or more emotionally laden slogans to spread troublesome dissension.

Accusing - makes judgmental accusations.

Spying - may follow the pastor, tape-record telephone conversations.

Distorting - frequently distorts incidents, leaving grains of truth to maintain credibility.

Misquoting Scripture - to provide proof that their campaigns or behaviors are legitimate.

Judas Kissing - might say, "I am your friend, but.." A church leader once may have thought the antagonist was a special friend.

Smirking - might wear an inappropriate smile or cocky grin when he or she encounters the person under attack.

Pestering - calling on the phone or by hanging around after the service or meeting, saying, "I'd like a brief word with you."

Letter writing - sending letters or other communication.

Pretense - portraying themselves as champions of the underdog, or as victims themselves.

Lobbying - lobby with small groups in the church to create doubt about leaders.

PREVENTING ANTAGONISM:

Follow your denomination's established policies and procedures. Keep your District Superintendent informed about people who are stirring up strife in the congregation.

It is wise for a pastor to establish functional feedback channels, such as a group of elders or deacons. Some churches have created a pastor prayer support team that gives advice and works to protect their pastor from unfair criticism.

Job descriptions avoid infringement onto another's responsibility. This helps prevent bossy individuals from overstepping the bounds of respect toward other volunteers and disregarding the efforts of others.

Establish broad based ministry teams that emphasize shared responsibility and the inclusion of everyone.

Discipline that works discourages antagonists from avoiding accountability and will cause them to hesitate in challenging standard operational procedures.

Anticipatory socialization – this means requiring volunteers to keep the church leadership informed about their plans and activities.

A united leadership front frustrates the antagonist who attempts to "divide & conquer." A smart antagonist will try to cast doubt into the mind of the easily swayed.

RELATING TO DORMANT ANTAGONISTS:

Act professionally by being consistent, responsible and self-controlled.

Keep your distance. "Do not throw your pearls before swine, lest they trample them under foot, and turn and attack you." (Matthew 7:6)

Be accurate, don't guess or give any off-the-cuff opinions. Choose your words carefully.

Avoid excessive positive reinforcement when they do something commendable.

Tighten the reins. Discourage the antagonist's involvement in leadership.

Don't seek empathy from others. Try not to whine.

Don't form a committee to look into accusations; this only appears to give credibility to their concerns.

Don't call for a vote of confidence. It forces people to take sides. Display self-confidence.

All church leaders, especially the pastor-revitalizer, must be willing to help the congregation become healthy. Some of the sick we encounter in a dying church are wounded, angry, lonely, antagonists who are in need of God's love. Even though the pastor tries to help the antagonist to the best of his ability, he cannot sacrifice the congregation to the whims of one individual who waves his money and practices selfish control. We practice the love of Christ and treat everyone in the congregation the same. This means that we care enough about the future of our church not to allow anyone to stifle its ability to liberate people from bondage or victimization. It means that we care enough about the bully that we will not allow the bully to intimate the church because we know the spiritual vitality of both the bully and the church is at stake.

CHAPTER 8 THE PASTOR AS LEADER

I have read extensively about leadership. I believe that leadership is essential to bringing any church to growth and vitality. The next two chapters look into pastoral leadership and "change agent" leadership.

In high school, I wasn't in charge of anything. Like most students, I was not voted to an office, or asked to head up a task. I recall being nominated to be the Science Club president. No one voted for me, including the guy who nominated me! Apparently, I didn't impress my classmates. I realize that is a silly example, but it is the sort of experience that causes you to question your leadership potential.

When I became a pastor, I attended every John Maxwell seminar I could. Over the years, I have read a lot about leadership and my library is stocked with books on the subject. I wondered if I was a leader or not. Can I learn leadership? Are leaders born with the ability to lead or can one be trained? How do I ascertain whether I am a leader or not? What does a leader look like? What do capable leaders have in common? This chapter is a result of my search for answers.

The successful organization has one major attribute that sets it apart from unsuccessful organizations: dynamic and effective leadership. We can agree that the role of pastoral leadership in church revitalization is crucial, but it invites the obvious question: What is leadership?

It is said that the Library of Congress has 10,000 books on the subject and there are probably an equal number of leadership consultants. It was Warren Bennis, a top specialist in the field of leadership, who first estimated that there are over 350 definitions of the term "leadership." Here is a sampling of those definitions:

> Leadership is the combination of traits that enable a particular individual to motivate others to accomplish given tasks.

> Leadership is the process by which one individual consistently exerts more impact than others on the nature and direction of the group.

Leadership is making things happen that wouldn't ordinarily happen.

Leadership is the ability to decide what is to be done and then do it.

Leadership is working with and through individuals to accomplish organizational goals.

Leadership is the wise use of power used to achieve results through people.

Leadership is doing with and through others what needs to be done to accomplish an objective.

The purpose of this chapter is to look at what some have said about leadership and to apply common leadership principles to pastoral ministry, as it relates to revitalization and church growth from a Biblical perspective. Leadership presupposes that the person in charge is a person who makes things happen. Former president of Columbia University, Nicholas Murray Butler, said, "There are three kinds of people in the world - those who don't know what's happening, those who watch what's happening, and those who make things happen." He continues,

> Though leadership may be hard to define, the one characteristic common to all leaders is the ability to make things happen - to act in order to help others work in an environment within which each individual serving under him finds himself encouraged and stimulated to a point where he is helped to realize his fullest potential to contribute meaningfully.

The pastor-leader should not step aside when his church is looking for him to step up. Those called by God have always been people of action. Their faith is connected to striving toward a goal. "When God creates a leader, He gives him the capacity to make things happen", or as Richard Wolfe points out, "when God creates a leader he is given a volition for action." When a congregation is struggling to survive, the last thing they need is a passive person who was not called to their situation. John Maxwell says that, "The leaders in any organization must be the environmental change agents."

The pastor may not have all the answers but he should have some of the qualities of leadership or at least be willing to learn how to lead. People are willing follow a leader when they perceive that they will benefit from the interchange. There are qualities that leaders can develop that will enhance their chances for being followed.

Why leadership is desired. What kind of leadership is the most desirable in a pastor? Warren Bennis suggests that the best leaders empower those under him or her. The effectiveness of leadership is seen in the lives of the followers. This is a major theme among pastors who focus on equipping volunteers. If leaders are effectively empowering followers, here is what happens:

> People feel significant. Everyone feels that he or she makes a difference to the success of the organization.

> Learning and competence matter. Leaders value learning and mastery, and so do people who work with them.

> People are part of a community. Where there is leadership, there is a team, a family, a unity.

> Work is exciting. Where there are leaders, work is stimulating, challenging, fascinating and fun.

Emotional intelligence. Ideally, a minister will have been trained at a seminary and will have the spiritual gifting necessary for leading a group of people. Daniel Goleman believes that in addition to analytical and technical skills, the most effective leaders have one crucial ingredient in their leadership mix: a high degree of "emotional intelligence". He says that emotional intelligence may be the key trait that distinguishes outstanding leaders from mediocre ones. Emotional intelligence is a combination of self-management skills and the ability to work with others.

According to Goleman, there are five components to emotional intelligence: self-awareness, self-regulation, motivation, empathy, and social skill. In the field of leadership development, Goleman's research and writings are highly regarded as reviewed by Bill Easum, who said,

In his groundbreaking book, *Emotional Intelligence*, Daniel Goleman performs a great service to the field of leadership. I have always believed that passion is the most important trait of any effective leader, but I did not know why until I read this book. Goleman's conclusion is that emotional intelligence matters more in leadership than IQ.

Below is a discussion of how each of the five components of emotional intelligence fits into the leadership qualities of the revitalizer-pastor.

The first component is self-awareness. According to Goleman, self-awareness means having a deep understanding of one's emotions, strengths, weaknesses, needs, and drives. People with strong self-awareness are neither overly critical nor unrealistically hopeful. Rather, they are honest with themselves and others. Below are more characteristics of self-awareness.

> Self-awareness extends to a person's understanding of his or her values and goals.

> Self-awareness shows itself as candor and an ability to assess oneself realistically.

> Self-aware people recognize how their feelings affect them, other people, and their job performance.

> Self-aware people know and are comfortable talking about their limitations and strengths, and they often demonstrate a thirst for constructive criticism.

> Self-aware people are recognized by their self-confidence. They have a firm grasp of their capabilities and are less likely to set themselves up to fail. They know when to ask for help.

A healthy pastor will have realistic expectations of himself. If a pastor is not honest about his limitations he may attempt to do more than he ought rather than delegate responsibility to others. Ministers do not like to turn down requests because they do not want to be seen as uncaring, even if the appeal is outside of their spiritual gifting. A self-aware pastor will be able to say "no" and be able to explain why.

The pastor-revitalizer has a realistic assessment of his strengths and may surprise people with his self-depreciating humor, which communicates self-confidence. Jim Herrington says that leaders should be able to conduct an honest self-assessment:

> The leaders of effective transformations are honest with God and with themselves. They understand that the best way to lead their congregations, particularly through challenging times, is to have a realistic understanding of their own capabilities and shortcomings. Therefore, they spend time looking at their motives, fears, gifts, and faults. This self-assessment should clarify how they tend to lead, where they will need help, and what pitfalls they should seek to avoid.

The second component is self-regulation. Self-regulation, which is like an ongoing inner conversation, is the component of emotional intelligence that frees us from being prisoners of our feelings.

> People who are in control of their feelings and impulses - that is, people who are reasonable - are able to create an environment of trust and fairness. Fewer bad moods at the top mean fewer throughout the organization. People who have mastered their emotions are able to roll with the changes.

Emotional health is extremely vital. Pastors suffer burnout at an alarming rate and leave the ministry every year as they suffer from loneliness, isolation, and feelings of inadequacy. There is great emotional pressure in the ministry for a variety of reasons. Gloom and depression can lead to uncontrolled anger and may exhibit itself through outbursts, hasty judgments, abuse of power, or personal attacks on others. Ted Engstrom noted that,

> Persons really in touch with themselves make the best leaders. If the leader senses he is immature or unstable, he should seek to improve himself. As one changes and enlarges his capacity to appreciate and relate to others, his personality is enriched. When this happens, the intellect and emotions become keener and more perceptive. The result is a warmer, more responsive and aware human being who is in tune with others in his feelings.

Change is not easy for a congregation and change is not easy for a pastor. "Before we can change the way we act, we have to change the way we feel and think. We have to change our image of reality. We have to change the way we perceive the church." In order to change his thinking, a pastor needs to be open to working outside his comfort zone and consider ministry from different perspectives. Maxwell notes that, "Effective leaders recognize that their emotional reactions are their own responsibility. A leader who decides not to allow other people's actions to dictate his reactions experiences an empowering freedom."

Pastors are held to a different standard than other people. Parishioners may not accept that their pastor needs to visit a Christian counselor who can help him understand his emotions. For example, unregulated anger is damaging within the church fellowship, especially when it is displayed by the pastor when circumstances are beyond his control. "People who have mastered their emotions are able to roll with the changes. They don't panic." Negative emotions that trickle down from the pastor may give people reason for pause.

> The signs of emotional self-regulation, therefore, are not hard to miss: a propensity for reflection and thoughtfulness; comfort with ambiguity and change; and integrity - an ability to say no to impulsive urges. In my research, extreme displays of negative emotion have never emerged as a driver of good leadership.

The third component is motivation. A pastor who is called by God to serve in a church usually has great motivation. He is a self-starter and he has a passion for his work. As Goleman comments, "When people love their job for the work itself, they often feel committed to the organizations that makes that work possible." When a pastor is driven by a vision, there are goals that he wants to attain. The result is that he will stay the course. Because a motivated leader works hard and has a strong vision, he inspires followers to expect great things to happen.

> If there is one trait that virtually all effective leaders have, it is motivation. They are driven to achieve beyond expectations -

their own and everyone else's...those with leadership potential are motivated by a deeply embedded desire to achieve for the sake of achievement...such people seek out creative challenges, love to learn, and take great pride in a job well done. They also display an unflagging energy to do things better.

The fourth component is empathy. Empathy means thoughtfully considering people's feelings, along with other factors, in the process of making intelligent decisions. Warren Bennis said that, "Leading through voice, inspiring through trust and empathy does more than get people on your side. It can change the climate enough to give people elbow room to do the right things." Empathy allows a pastor to understand the emotional makeup of key people in the church. Listening to people's concerns shows respect for their views and allows for open dialogue. Listening is a powerful communication tool that is not practiced enough by leaders. Stephen Covey observes,

> We typically seek first to be understood. Most people do not listen with the intent to understand; they listen with the intent to reply. They're either speaking or preparing to speak. They're filtering everything through their own paradigms, reading their autobiography into people's lives.

The pastor's empathy is appreciated because it shows that he cares enough to ask others' opinion and that he values member's participation in the decision making process. This results in a sense of team unity.

The fifth component is social skill. Any leader who is gifted at building relationships has an advantage when it come to team building. If there is anything that a pastor must have it is people skills. Few professions require a person to have so many points of contact. Members in a congregation can choose who they talk to, but the pastor is expected to be gracious to everyone who enters the fellowship.

The word gets around quickly when a pastor is considered unapproachable. Friendliness is a characteristic that congregants expect the pastor to possess. "Excellent people skills involve a genuine concern for others, the ability to understand people, and the decision to make positive interaction with others a primary concern. A successful leader knows this."

The revitalizing pastor will most likely have the ability to meet new people and develop the types of friendships that he can draw on as he introduces change. He is a people-person and a coalition builder who has convinced the influencers of his sincerity and authenticity. Instead of disputing over trivial matters, he looks for areas of agreement while working toward his larger vision. Regarding social skills, Maxwell notes,

> Social Skill - is friendliness with a purpose: moving people in the direction you desire. Social skilled people tend to have a wide circle of acquaintances, and they have the knack for finding common ground with people of all kinds - a knack for building rapport. The leader's task is to get work done through other people, and social skill makes that possible.

When a pastor finds common ground and builds rapport with members, he creates confidence and respect for his views. The characteristics of a leader possessing social skills are good communication skills, cooperativeness, sociability, personal integrity, and the ability to influence others.

Leadership principles. Just as there is no clear definition of leadership, there are no clear principles of leadership, either. Each leader brings to bear certain qualities that are unique to him. The Bible clearly points this out in Hebrews 11. The leaders mentioned here are as different in character as are the situations in which they find themselves. Applying the principles of leadership is a matter of who you are and what leadership approach is best for you.

It is similar to a pastor trying to find his preaching style. He can read all the books in the world about preaching, but he still must discover what works for him. A number of factors including his personality, education, and background determine his style of preaching. Billy Graham does not preach like David Wilkerson, and David Wilkerson does not preach like Chuck Swindoll or T.D. Jakes. Although each man would agree that a preacher must be called by God, each man is comfortable with his own style, delivery, and ministry. Just as ministers preach with different styles, people lead in different ways. Michael Porter made this point in a speech he gave to a group of aspiring leaders.

> I learned that early in my career at American Motors when I tried to emulate the tough, forceful management style of an executive I admired. While that approach was effective for him, it wasn't comfortable for me because it didn't suit my personality. As a consequence, I was inconsistent. I'd forget to put on my "tough face". This was confusing and frustrating for others because they couldn't be sure which Michael would appear from moment to moment.

I like the leadership principles espoused by Michael Porter because they resonate with my personality. Porter gives his audience latitude, "There is no formula for becoming an effective leader. If you took the time to sort through all of it, I'm quite certain one truth would emerge - leadership means different things to different people." Porter makes seven recommendations based on his personal experience:

> *Develop your own leadership style.* What works for me may not work for you.

> *Build a shared vision.* That means understanding where you are today, where you want to be tomorrow, why, and how you're going to get there.

> *Coach, Motivate, Facilitate.* Leaders get others to reach beyond themselves.

> *Celebrate the small stuff.* Acknowledge team efforts. Applaud successes.

> *Advocate life-long learning.* Life-long learning is energizing. It's liberating. It opens doors to new opportunities.

> *Take risks, embrace change.* Don't be afraid to try new things. Don't fear failure. Change is never ending.

> *Lead by example.* Leaders influence less by what they say than by what they do.

Leadership qualities. John Maxwell has developed a list of important qualities to look for in a leader:

Character - some of the qualities that make up good character include honesty, integrity, self-discipline, teach-ability, perseverance, conscientiousness, and a strong work ethic.

Influence - the quality of the follower will indicate the quality of the leader. Are his followers positive producers or a bunch of mediocre yes-men?

Positive Attitude - the person doesn't accept the normal limitations of life as most people do. People with positive attitudes are able to go places where others can't. They do things others can't. They are not restricted by self-imposed limitations.

Excellent People Skills - a leader without people skills soon has no followers. People skills involve a genuine concern for others, the ability to understand people, and the decision to make positive interaction with others a primary concern.

Evident Gifts - Every person God creates has gifts. Someone with raw talent (gifts) but few skills for harnessing that ability needs training. Once he is given help developing those skills, he will begin to become the person he was created to be.

Proven Track Record - a leader always has a proven record of accomplishment. Everyone who breaks new ground, who strives to do something, makes mistakes. People without proven track records either haven't learned from their mistakes or haven't tried anything new.

Confidence - people are naturally attracted to people who convey confidence. Confidence is characteristic of a positive attitude. The greatest achievers and leaders remain confident regardless of circumstances.

Self-Discipline - when it comes to self-discipline, people choose one of two things: the pain of discipline, which comes from sacrifice and growth, or the pain of regret, which comes from the easy road and missed opportunities.

Effective Communication Skills - Without the ability to communicate, a leader cannot effectively cast his vision and call his people to act on that vision. Liking people is the beginning of the ability to communicate. He has a genuine concern for the person he's talking to, the ability to focus on the responder, good eye contact, and a warm smile.

Discontent With the Status Quo - leaders see what is, but more important, they have a vision for what could be. They are never content with things as they are. A leader who loves the status quo soon becomes a follower.

So, what is leadership? Although there are many definitions of leadership, we can say one thing: leaders lead. As simple as this may sound, leaders are those people who get things done. The leader does not sit around waiting for someone else to lead. When they see the objective, they go for it. They may not know exactly how they are going to proceed, but they do know who is in charge. For me, leadership is doing the right thing because it is the right thing to do. It says, "Here's what we are going to do, this is why we are going to do it, and this is how we are going to do it."

The movie, "Sergeant York", is one of my favorite movies. It is the story of Alvin C. York, a young Christian conscientious objector who, after great moral deliberation, decided to fight in World War I. In the crucial scene that made him famous, York's commanding officer is wounded by machine gun fire and tells Corporal York that he is now "in charge". York looks around and sees that five German machine gun nests have killed hundreds of American men and many more would die. The extraordinary marksman immediately took action. Grabbing two pistols and his rifle, he begins to crawl around all the dead bodies in order to get a better shot at the Germans. His commanding officer, seeing the audacity of his plan yells, "York, get back here. You'll get killed." York only replies, "Sorry sir, but you already put me in charge." When he was done, York had single-handedly eliminated all five machine guns nests and captured 132 German prisoners.

Later, when he asked why he did it, he simply said. "I saw all those men getting killed and I decided that somebody had to do something. So, I did." Engstrom states, "Men of faith have always been men of action. It is an impossibility for active men to serve in a passive role. This implies that such people are decisive in nature. Leadership action demands faith. The setting and striving for goals is an act of faith."

Taking action means that the leader has a plan. A pastor with leadership qualities will have a vision, goals, and a time line. He will equip and train his church for future growth and develop them for ministry. He appreciates organization and knows that he needs people with administrative gifts to help him arrange his teams to perform specific tasks. He has an awareness of what is going on. He practices the art of delegation and spurs the people around him to action. He knows that failing to plan is planning to fail.

What is leadership? I think Ted Engstrom sums up what leadership is from a Christian perspective:

> The concept of leader means one who guides activities of others and who himself acts and performs to bring those activities about. He is capable of performing acts that will guide a group in achieving objectives. He takes the capacities of vision and faith, has the ability to be concerned and comprehend, exercises action through effective and personal influence in the direction of an enterprise and the development of the potential into practical and/or profitable means. To accomplish this, a true leader must have a strong drive to take the initiative to act - a kind of initial stirring that causes people and an organization to use their best abilities to accomplish a desired end.

CHAPTER 9 THE "CHANGE AGENT" PASTOR

"The ultimate measure of a man is not where he stands in moments of comfort and convenience, but where he stands at time of challenge and controversy." ~ Martin Luther King

"Society is changing at a faster rate than ever before. Because of this, the church of Christ must be willing to change its methods if it is to remain relevant. The challenge is to change the methods, which are temporal, without changing the message, which is timeless. Many within the church resist change for fear of compromising the message of Christ. For this reason, the 21st-century pastor must see himself as a change agent that can implement effective changes while making them palatable to church members." ~ Randy Helms

The change agent pastor is a leader. If any congregation is to experience change that leads to growth, the pastor needs a certain amount of leadership potential. A person can take all the courses, have all the technical skills associated with pastoral ministry, receive a diploma, be given a title and a congregation, and not be a leader. It is troubling that few pastors who are seminary graduates have had leadership training or possess leadership abilities. In addition, there is a shortage of pastors in some denominations, thereby placing individuals in the pulpit who may not be effective as pastors. Why is this? First, it is possible that some seminarians are not be called by God to be pastors. Second, because there are too few pastors, a church can become desperate and hire someone who is not called by God to pastor. Third, small churches cannot afford quality leaders with a track record of revitalization. As a result, few congregations are experiencing growth.

In his book, *Courageous Leadership*, Bill Hybels, laments the lack of change in the local church and believes the reason is the lack of leadership in the pulpit. There are churches that do not see the need to reach out and have an impact on their community.

> These good people, and hundreds of thousands of others like them in churches all over the world, have never been led. They've been preached to and taught. They've been

fellowshipped and Bible-studied. They've taken courses on prayer and evangelism. But with no one to inspire them, to mobilize them, and to coordinate their efforts, their desire to make a difference for Christ has been completely frustrated.

Just what kind of leadership is needed in today's non-growing church? That of a change agent or catalyst. In *Church Growth Principles*, Kirk C. Hadaway explains,

> The type of leadership which seems to best characterize the pastors of breakout churches is that of the catalyst. The catalyst creates an organizational atmosphere in which positive goals are reached and people are being built up. It is the most effective style because it has a positive impact on the church as an organization and on individual members. Goals are established; members feel ownership because they had a hand in the development of the goals; and they are motivated to reach the goals.

These pastors are "change agents" in the particular situation where God has placed them. They are inspirational, go-get-'em types, who see a need and set out to keep a sinking ship from sinking. They roll up their sleeves and get to work. They love the challenge, especially when the situation looks impossible. They are not passive people who wait for someone to tell them what to do. The change agent pastor, the revitalizer, must attempt to break the old mold and introduce a new one. His diplomatic skills will assist him as he convinces the established members in the church to consider his ideas and head in a different direction.

One sign that a church has benefited from having a change agent pastor is found in the domino effect. A congregation is languishing, calls a change agent pastor, then about two years later word spreads that "good things are happening at that church." The members have a new sense of excitement attendance is up. Kirk Hadaway describes the results of a church revitalized,

> No longer did members have to apologize for the sorry state of their church; no longer did they suffer through having to call a new pastor every two years; no longer did they wait weeks and

weeks before someone was saved or someone joined the church. The church had suddenly become fun and a source of pride; their pastor was not about to leave the church in the midst of its revival; and the testimonies of new members had become a weekly occurrence. This is the catalytic role at its best.

The change agent pastor is a risk taker. Taking risks is scary. It takes courage. When the pastor enters a struggling church, there is nowhere to go but up. After all, what is there to lose? There is a reason behind the church's slow disintegration and he will eventually discover it. What happens when he does? Is the pastor willing to do what is necessary? As Larry Osborne observed: "The most striking thing about highly effective leaders is how little they have in common. What one swears by, another warns against. But one trait stands out: the willingness to risk." The pastor must be willing to say, "Sorry, guys, but we may need to approach some things differently. I would like to introduce some ideas that you may want to consider. Some things need to change." Warren Bennis said it so well, "Managers are people who do things right and leaders are people who the right thing."

Just mentioning the word "change" is a risk, especially to those who have been taught the non-proactive servant-leadership pastor model. John Maxwell connects risk taking to courage, especially when making tough decisions. He presents these truths about courage:

Courage begins with an inward battle. Courage is not an absence of fear. It is doing what you are afraid to do.

Courage is making things right, not just smoothing them over.

Courage deals with principle, not perception. Your dedication to potential must remain stronger than your desire to appease others.

Courage in a leader inspires commitment from followers. A show of courage by any person encourages others. But a show of courage by a leader inspires.

Your life expands in proportion to your courage. Fear limits a leader. Courage not only gives you a good beginning, but it

91

also provides for a better future.

Maxwell continues with another truth about courage and taking risks,

> What is ironic is that those who don't have the courage to take risks and those who do experience the same amount of fear in life. The only difference is that those who don't take chances worry about trivial things. If you're going to have to overcome your fear and doubts anyway, you might as well make it count.

According to John Miller,

> The key question is, Do you have the courage of faith to think through the issues - to discern God's will for your congregation? My concern is that recognizing the risks may keep you from doing anything about the ingrown church. But I believe that discerning risk-taking is essential to the healthy growth of church leaders and congregations. As leaders and member of churches we are continually faced with a choice: either take risks or rust where you are. Often, I believe, our problem as leaders is that we have unconsciously chosen to rust where we are, because of the fear of failing or losing our dignity. We need to accept the reality that every ministry that is from God will have some failures in it. We must make the mistakes that go with maturing or we cannot become an effective leader in Christ's sheepfold. We must be willing to take a risk every time we preach a sermon with daring and specific applications.

The change agent pastor must work on the "edge", which means he must be courageous when the time comes to make decisions. He must seek the truth, find the reality of the situation, and base his decisions on the truth available to him. There will be times when he will need to set his emotions aside and have the courage to act on the truth and make tough calls.

Often, in non-growth environments, a creative pastor will hear what some have referred to as "killer phrases", which come from people who are afraid of risk and prefer to play it safe, hindering change in a positive direction. In his forty years in Christian leadership, Charles Swindoll lists killer phrases that he has heard ruin meetings and brainstorming settings:

> It won't work.
>
> We haven't the time.
>
> We don't have the personnel to pull it off.
>
> It's not in the budget.
>
> We're going to get too much attention.
>
> The board isn't going to buy it.
>
> We've tried that before.
>
> We've never done that before.
>
> We're not ready for it yet.
>
> We'll lose a lot of high donors if we do that.
>
> All right in theory, but can you put it into practice?
>
> This could result in a lawsuit.
>
> It's too modern.
>
> It's too old fashioned.
>
> So and so tried that and failed.
>
> We're too small for that.
>
> We're too big for that.
>
> It costs too much money.
>
> People won't accept it.

However, a pastor needs to use wisdom regarding his goals, because flexibility is needed when things do not work out according to our plan. We need to avoid becoming so stubborn that those around us are unable to have input, or warn us, about possible dangers in our risk taking ideas. Charles Swindoll, in his book about the life of *Joseph*, made this observation:

A leader must be wise and flexible, willing to give here and there, willing to delegate, willing to listen to alternative plans and ideas of those alongside. Everything doesn't have to be your way. You are responsible for the oversight and the direction, but that does not mean you have the right to squelch every bit of the innovation. Many a church or organization has lost people exactly because of this kind of inflexibility. As an employee, Joseph was loyal, accountable, wise, objective, and efficient. As a leader, he was efficient, wise, objective, and flexible. There was also a quiet and secure calmness in his leadership that is beautiful to watch.

The change agent pastor is a transformational leader. Leadership is the key factor in all successful ministries. Everything rises and falls on leadership. There is a difference between a pastor who maintains the status quo of an existing, non-growing congregation, and a leader who is a change agent - a spark plug. Most people agree that it takes a gutsy individual to turn around a floundering church. The change agent pastor is a transformational leader. As Leith Anderson observes,

> He is a driven by a vision of a new tomorrow, wins supporters and followers for that vision, and transforms the congregation. The change from growing older and smaller to growing younger and larger represents radical change, discontinuity, and requires a new set of priorities. It is a transformation. This often reflected in the comment of the old timer who observes, "It sure is different here from when I joined thirty years ago."

A transformational leader will take action as quickly as possible because he knows that the last thing a dying church needs is a man of indecision and inaction. Transformation is what the church must have if it is to rise out of its downward spiral. The change agent pastor is Holy Spirit filled and led to inspire the discouraged people to dream dreams and see visions of what God can do at their church.

According to Leith Anderson, in *Dying for Change,* the transformational leader has four characteristics that directly change a church. First, "transformational leaders stay close to the action. If leaders allow themselves to become isolated in the problems and perspectives of leadership, they lose touch with those whom they claim to lead." Pastors who refuse to recognize paradigm shifts have probably lost contact with the society they are reaching out to and do not understand why their past ministry style is ineffective.

Second, "transformational leaders get authority from followers." New pastors often make the mistake of thinking that just because they graduated from seminary or have a title that they have authority. People will follow only those whom they choose to follow. There is a difference between leading with power and having authority. Power is something we have over someone else to make them do what they do not want to do. Authority is earned trust and confidence in one's ability to lead. As John Maxwell has noted, "When a person gains authority through position, he lays hold of the title by rights. People follow him because they have to. Do not falsely assume when you are voted into a church that you earned the congregation's allegiance." When a leader has authority, people will want to follow. Long-term pastors often have authority because the congregation has learned that they can depend on them.

Third, "transformational leaders excel amid adversity." They know that the situation might get worse before it gets better. Anyone can lead when times are very good. But, what happens when criticism comes the pastor's way?

Fourth, "transformational leaders take the initiative." Transformational leaders diagnose the situation, motivate the church, get people involved, and expect God to do great works among them. They are risk takers and people of action.

Kirk Hadaway notes that, "Catalytic pastors are friendly, vigorous, optimistic, flexible, and persistent. They know what they want to happen, but they understand the axiom, 'never use a bullwhip when a smile will do.' Things happen in their churches because they know how to delegate and motivate." The pastor comes in with a positive attitude and assumes that good things are going to happen. His excitement is infectious and spreads throughout the congregation. "The type of leadership which seems to best characterize the pastors of breakout churches is that of the catalyst. The catalyst creates an organizational atmosphere in which positive goals are reached and people are being built up."

Gary McIntosh, writing in his book, *One Size Does Not Fit All*, has come to the same conclusion about the magnitude of pastoral leadership in regard to church growth.

> Since the early 1970s a large number of studies have been conducted on growing churches in North America. A persistent thread running through all this research has been the need for a high caliber of pastoral leadership. Second only to the empowering work of the Holy Spirit, pastoral leadership is the most determinative factor in growing churches. Any church that desires to develop a healthy ministry must adequately recognize that strong pastoral competence is a decisive factor for the vitality and outreach of their congregation.

Leadership has always been the pivotal force behind any successful organization. Leadership is what gives a church its vision and the ability to translate that vision into reality. Bill Hybels has concluded that the Bible supports strong leadership, "As I've looked through the Scriptures at those who throughout history have been unmistakably strong leaders, I've noticed certain behavior patterns and attitudes that they hold in common." According to Hybels, eight Biblical characteristics have important implications for the local church:

> Leaders have the ability to cast vision.
>
> Leaders have the ability to coalesce people.
>
> Leaders have the ability to inspire and motivate people.
>
> Leaders are able to identify the need for positive change and then bring it about.
>
> Leaders establish core values.
>
> Leaders allocate resources effectively.
>
> Leaders have the ability to identify entropy.

Leaders love to create a leadership culture.

The impact of leadership, as listed by Hybels, is invaluable to keeping the local church on track and moving in a forward direction. It is unwise for congregations to disregard the gift of pastoral leadership, especially when it comes to turning a church around. A leader is going to need dynamic skills, which includes the persona of an influencing motivator. Some writers, like Kirk Hadaway, seem to bemoan the fact that strong leaders have charismatic personalities.

> Super church pastors are unusual individuals, many with great personal charisma and preaching gifts. Much of what they have done is because of who they are, and that cannot be copied. So rather than focusing on these churches, research should look at a wide range of growing churches, plateaued churches, and declining churches to discover if there are any characteristics held by growing church pastors which sets them apart from the pastors of churches which are not growing.

The change agent pastor prepares others for ministry. There is growth potential when the pastor is a strong leader who wants the church to grow and is willing to pay the price, and the congregation is willing to let the pastor lead and is motivated for growth. Part of the pastor's role is to prepare and train others for service. The pastor should not be expected to do all the work himself. He supports the gifts of others and looks for ways for the church to benefit from them.

Pastor Wayne Cordeiro once said, "No one person is meant to carry this assignment [a divine purpose] alone. It wasn't designed that way. We were created to do church as a team! A full symphony under the direction of a master conductor will always sound infinitely better than a one man band." Peter Wagner drives home this point,

> The chief contribution of the laypeople to the growth of the church can be summed up in one word: ministry. This is taught clearly in the Bible. Pastors, along with other leaders such as apostles, prophets, evangelists and teachers, were given by God to the church for the specific function of: "equipping of the saints for the work of ministry". Every church member is supposed to be an active minister...we should not think of a

church as a group with one or two ministers, but rather as a group in which every one is a minister.

The change agent pastor appreciates the long-range development of equipping and mobilizing Christians for service. He knows that it takes God's power and the involvement of others using their God-given gifts to build a healthy church. Equipping means sharing vision, selecting leaders, forming teams, creating communication mechanisms that help people prepare for future ministry opportunities.

> To see ourselves as player-coach and not as the whole team frees the conscience from a sense of endless obligation. We abandon the idea that we are the head of the church, the owner of the family of God, and once we let go in this way, we discover that people will follow us much more readily. The work of equipping and discipling consists of two elements in the New Testament: the pastor equips God's people (1) by teaching them the gospel, and (2) by training then to use their spiritual gifts to serve Christ.

What makes an equipping pastor unusual is their sense of urgent need and the wisdom to know that it will take as many people as possible to get the work done. He will have a mission that is inspiring and clearly worth achieving, and goals that will stretch people's abilities. He is a highly motivated leader who is optimistic that the situation is going to improve because he believes that it will. Motivation is an important factor in the life of the leader. Daniel Goleman, in his article, "*What Makes a Leader*", wrote,

> Interestingly, people with high motivation remain optimistic even when the score is against them. It's not difficult to understand how and why a motivation to achieve translates into strong leadership. If you set the performance bar high for yourself, you will do the same for the organization when you are in a position to do so. Likewise, a drive to surpass goals and an interest in keeping score can be contagious. Leaders with these traits can often build a team of managers around them with the same traits.

The leader's challenge is to create a spirit of teamwork that says, "We're all in this together", and a realistic expectation that the team members can meet the goal. Training and equipping does not occur overnight. A pastor cannot stay for a short period and expect to see long-term results. The pastor wishing to see a church turn around will know that developing lay leaders and establishing a vision for growth takes time.

The change agent pastor prepares for change. The Church in the United States is going to change in ways that may not be predicted. The innovative ministries of today may not be effective in the next generation. Just as there have been cultural and generational differences in the church in the past, the generation of Baby Boomers will need to make some adjustments as they near retirement. The younger, non-boomer pastors, commonly referred to as "Millennials" and "Baby Busters", will have ideas of their own but will have to deal with the aging flock of Baby Boomers, and this will not be easy. Bennis once remarked, "The leader may discover that the culture of his own corporation is an obstacle to the changes he wants to introduce, because as currently constituted, it is more devoted to preserving itself than meeting new challenges." Hopefully, Baby Boomers will recall what it was like trying to convince their parents to make changes in the church and will be more flexible for their children.

The "Truman Generation", those who were teenagers during President Truman's administration, have been turning over the leadership reins to their children. Their Baby Boomer children struggled with the apparatus of the church set up by their grandparents and parents. The Baby Boomers ushered in the rock and roll influence in the worship service, informal dress, and contemporary translations of the Bible. They are more than happy to be in control of the church. Some questions to consider are: What will be the state of the local congregation when the Baby Boomers fill most of the leadership positions? Will they allow the generation after them to have a say? So much has been written about attracting Baby Boomers, but what will the revitalizing pastor encounter when it is the Boomers' turn to change paradigms? Will the Baby Boomers be open to change or will they like their parents and hinder church growth? There may come a time when the change agent pastors of the next generation will need to revitalize the Baby Boomer congregation. Change, even good change, is threatening to some members. Nevertheless, as one layperson said in a once-stagnant, rural church in Arkansas, "It's hard to argue with folks being saved." There is nothing like success to calm the uneasiness of old members, especially when people are coming to Christ.

While there are churches that are exploding in size, the end of the smaller congregation is not in sight. The small church may attract the younger baby-busters because they are more likely to yearn for a closer fellowship. Pollster George Barna says, "Younger people drop out of church because they struggle to find a place. They are one-third less likely than older adults to attend, give financially, or read the Bible." This comment sounds familiar. Every generation approaches church involvement differently than the one before.

> The smaller church is the right setting for many adults under age 35. Boomers like larger churches - one fourth attend churches of 500 or more, compared to one-sixth of busters. Barna credits the disinterest of busters in boomer-led organizations, and their desire for strong community. While some have predicted their demise, Barna says small congregations will remain prevalent. About 60 percent of U.S. churches have 100 or less in attendance each weekend.

There are many changes afoot in the way the churches in America organize to be effective. In order to provide the kind of ministries that people need we should to be open to adjusting our operating procedure. The church and the pastor will need to adapt to many unforeseen factors. Carl George gives four predictions in his book, *Prepare Your Church for the Future*:

First, we'll plan for an extended future. This means that the church should plan for the long term, instead of thinking that it does not need to plan because Jesus is coming back next week. He may, but we do not know. So, don't stop thinking about tomorrow!

Second, urban churches will set the pace. Metropolitan areas will become more concentrated in third world countries. "Not only will the typical church of the future be in the suburban shadow of some world-class city, but the people of that assembly will be non-white. I predict that churches of today represent the final generation of Western dominance in Christendom." This means that churches will need to reach out to where the people are.

Third, smaller churches will have part-time pastors. This is already the case in most rural churches. Denominational pastors often have two to three congregations for which they are responsible. No one church can pay for a full-time pastor.

Fourth, huge churches will be small enough to care. "The church of the future, though bigger than the typical parish of today, will not be known for its central meeting spot, but for its small group ministry." In other words, as the church grows larger it will grow smaller. George advocates a cell group "franchise" that reaches out to geographic areas.

CONCLUSION

Before congregational revitalization can occur, there must be an inner working of the Holy Spirit in the hearts and minds of the church members. Unless people experience a redemptive transformation, no amount of planning or skilled leadership will have a long-term impact. Only when people encounter the cross of Jesus Christ do they develop an authentic, loving community that cares for the lost. This requires that the pastor and congregational leaders be faithful followers of Jesus who devote their efforts to glorifying the Lord.

A congregation reflects the spiritual health of its prominent leaders and usually does not grow beyond their spiritual depth. "All this is from God, who reconciled us to himself through Christ and gave us the ministry of reconciliation: that God was reconciling the world to himself in Christ, not counting mens' sins against them. And he has committed to us the message of reconciliation. We are therefore Christ's ambassadors, as though God were making his appeal through us." (2 Corinthians 5:18-20)

The vital ingredient necessary for a congregation's revitalization and growth is a strong competent pastor with a vision and evangelistic focus. Effective revitalization requires a leader who can take the church in a forward direction. He is called by God to be the coach, the equipper, and the responsible leader who initiates change. As the revitalizing pastor, he is respectfully assertive as he challenges the status quo and helps the church to think out side the box. He is a perpetual student who recognizes that leadership requires continuous learning and skill development.

Rarely does a pastor possess all the abilities needed to walk the church through the change process. He knows that he will continuously need to equip people with the skills he does not have. He also looks for and trains new leaders. He builds his teams and emphasizes grace, and motivates them to live humbly with one another and serve others in love. As a result, they gladly serve through their spiritual gifts and build up the church body. "From Him the whole body, joined and held together by every supporting ligament, grows and builds itself up in love, as each part does its work." (Ephesians 4:16)

Each existing congregation has its own unique history, congregational make-up, and cultural complexities. The revitalizer appreciates that he is building on the work of others. "By the grace of God given me, I laid the foundation as an expert builder, and someone else is building on it. For no one can lay any foundation other than the one already laid, which is Jesus Christ." (1 Corinthians 3:10-11) There are proven church growth principles that can be applied universally to each church situation, as long as they are customized for the people in that particular setting. A skillful leader is flexible and tailors these principles to the cultural context of his congregation.

Growth can be encouraged and facilitated by providing the conditions wherein growth takes place, but we cannot make it happen. That is God's job. "So neither he who plants nor he who waters is anything, but only God, who makes things grow." (1 Corinthians 3:7) A church that works in cooperation with God's design will find itself growing. "For we are God's fellow workers; you are God's field, God's building." (1 Corinthians 3:9)

Everything must be done in the Lord's power and authority with the goal of honoring and pleasing Him. Growth will occur when we are more concerned that people encounter Jesus than that they have a good impression about our programs, our methods, our theological and philosophical bents, or us. Both the means and the end in growth must be filtered through the lens of Scripture. Just because a tactic or program seems to work does not mean it is of God. God will never violate what He has stated in His Word. The Word of God is the standard against which all is measured.

SOURCES CONSULTED

Anderson, Leith, *A Church for the 21st Century.; Dying for Change*; Armerding, Hudson T., *Leadership*; Augsburger, Myron S., Calvin Ratz, Frank Tillapaugh. *Mastering Outreach and Evangelism*; Avery, William O., *Revitalizing Congregations: Refocusing and Healing Through Transitions*; Axelrod, Alan, *Patton on Leadership (Strategic Lessons For Corporate Warfare);*.

Baker, Kenneth, General Editor, *The Holy Bible, The New International Version*; Barna, George, *Church Marketing; Leading Your Church Forward;; The Power of Vision; The Second Coming of the Church: A Blueprint for Survival; Turn-Around Churches*; *What Americans Believe: An Annual Survey of Values and Religious Views in the United States;* Bartel, Floyd G., *A New Look at Church Growth*; Bennis, Warren G., *On Becoming a Leader*; *Leaders: The Strategy for Taking Charge;* Buttry, Daniel, *Bring Your Church Back to Life: Beyond Survival Mentality*; Chaney, Charles L., *Church Planting at the End of the Twentieth Century*; Cho, Dr. Paul Y., *More Than Numbers*; Coleman, Robert E., *The Master Plan of Evangelism*; T*he Master Plan of Discipleship*; Compton, Stephen C., *Rekindling the Mainline: New Life Through New Church*;

Crandall, Ron, *Turn Around Strategies for the Small Church*; Covey, Stephen R., *The Seven Habits of Highly Effective People*; Dale, Bob, *Pastoral Leadership*; De Pree, Max, *Leading Without Power (Finding Hope In Serving Community)*; Easum, Bill, *Leadership on the Other Side: No Rule, Just Clues*; Engstrom, Ted, W., *The Making of a Christian Leader*; Ford, Leighton, *The Christian Persuader*; Freedman, David H., *Corps Business - The 30 Management Principles of the U.S. Marines*; Gangel, Kenneth O., Swindoll, Charles R., General Editor, *Coaching Ministry Teams; Feeding & Leading*, George, Carl F., *How to Break Growth Barriers*, and Robert F. Logan, *Leading & Managing Your Church*; *Prepare Your Church for Growth*; Hadaway, C. Kirk, *Church Growth Principles*, and Davis A. Roozen, *Rerouting the Protestant Mainstream*; Haugk, Kenneth C., *Antagonists in the Church (How to Identify and Deal with Destructive Conflict)*; Hemphill, Ken, *The Antioch Effect: 8 Characteristics of Highly Effective Churches;* Herrington, Jim; Bonem, Mike; Furr, James H.,

Leading Congregational Change: A Practical Guide for the Transformational Journey; Hower, Stephen D., *Sharpening the Sword (A Call to Strong and Courageous Leadership)*; Hunter, Kent R., *The Lord's Harvest and the Rural Church*; Hutcheson, Jr., Richard G., The *Wheel Within the Wheel: Confronting the Management Crisis of the Pluralistic Church*; Hybels, Bill and Lynn, *Rediscovering Church*; *Courageous Leadership*; Kotter, John P., *A Force for Change: How Leadership Differs from Management*; Kouzes, James M. and Posner, Barry Z., *The Leadership Challenge;* Logan, Robert E., *Beyond Church Growth*; London, H.B., and Neil Wiseman, *Pastors at Risk*; Mann, Alice, *Raising the Roof: The Pastoral-to-Program Transition*; Maxwell, John C., *Developing the Leaders Around You*, *Developing the Leader Within You*; *Failing Forward*, *The 21 Indispensable Qualities of a Leader*, McGavern, Donald A., *Understanding Church Growth*; McIntosh, Gary L., *One Size Does Not Fit All;* Miller, C. John, *Outgrowing the Ingrown Church*; Mullen, Thomas J., *The Renewal of the Ministry*; Ogden, Greg, *The New Reformation: Returning the Ministry to the People of God*, Pappas, Anthony G., *Entering the World of the Small Church*; Perry, Lloyd M., and Norman Shawchuck, Revitalizing the Twentieth-Century Church; Rainer, Thom S., *Eating the Elephant*; *Effective Evangelistic Churches*; Rendle, Gilbert R., *Leading Change in the Congregation*; Richards, Lawrence O., and Clyde Hoeldtke, *A Theology of Church Leadership*; Rutz, James H., *The Open Church*; Sanders, Oswald J., *Spiritual Leadership*; Schaller, Lyle E., *Activating the Passive Church*; *Effective Church Planting*; *The Small Church is Different*; Seel, John, *The Evangelical Forfeit*; Shenk, Wilbert R., *Exploring Church Growth*; Southerland, Dan, *Transitioning: Leading Your Church Through Change*, Snyder, Howard S., *The Community of the King*; Spader, Dann, and Gary Mayes, *Growing a Healthy Church*, Swindoll, Charles R., *Joseph*; Terry, John Mark, *Church Evangelism*; Towns, Elmer L., Peter C. Wagner, Thom S. Rainer, *The Everychurch Guide to Growth (How Any Plateaued Church Can Grow)*; *10 of Today's Most Innovative Churches*; *The Ten Greatest Revivals Ever*; Wagner, C. Peter, *Leading Your Church to Growth*; *Your Spiritual Gifts Can Help You Grow*; Warren, Rick, *The Purpose Driven Church*, Watson, David, *I Believe in Evangelism*, Wolfe, Richard, *Man at the Top*;

Yager, Dexter R., *Dynamic People Skills*; Young, Edwin B. and Andrew C. Stanley, *Can We Do That?*

Printed in Great Britain
by Amazon.co.uk, Ltd.,
Marston Gate.